Constructing Cooperation

Constructing Cooperation

*The Evolution of Institutions
of Comanagement*

Sara Singleton

Ann Arbor
THE UNIVERSITY OF MICHIGAN PRESS

2001   2000   1999   1998   4   3   2   1

A CIP catalog record for this book is available from the British Library.

Library of Congress Cataloging-in-Publication Data

Singleton, Sara (Sara G.)
    Constructing cooperation : the evolution of institutions of
comanagement / Sara Singleton.
        p.   cm.
    Includes bibliographical references and index.
    ISBN 0-472-10957-X (acid-free paper)
    1. Salmon fisheries—Northwest, Pacific.   2. Indians of North
America—Fishing—Northwest, Pacific.   3. Fishery
management—Northwest, Pacific.   I. Title.
SH348   .S57   1998
333.95'656'09795—dc21   98-19711
                                                        CIP

To Michael, with love

Contents

Illustrations

Acknowledgments

In preparing this book, I have benefited from the assistance of many people. The project began while I was in graduate school at the University of Washington, and I wish to thank the members of my dissertation committee—Donald McCrone (chair), Ellis Goldberg, and David Olson—for patience, praise, and constructive criticism in equal measure. Margaret Levi and Peter May provided helpful comments on early drafts. Yoram Barzel, whose course on property rights initially interested me in some of the issues explored herein, was kind enough to serve as graduate faculty representative. Dr. Gilbert Pauley, chair of the Fisheries Advisory Board, was helpful in the preliminary stages of the project. Many tribal and state fisheries managers were extremely generous with their time in explaining the intricacies of salmon ecology, state and federal regulation, and other matters related to piscatory practices. Such errors as remain are obviously my own responsibility.

Specifically, I wish to express my sincere gratitude to Larry Rutter, Gary Graves, Keith Lutz, Steve Robinson, and Craig Bowey of the Northwest Indian Fisheries Commission; Robert Turner (former director), Gene DiDonato, Pat Pattillo, Dana Mathews, Edward Manary, Larry Peck, Paul Sekulich, Teresa Scott, Anne Blakely, and Michael Fraidenburg of the Washington State Department of Fish and Wildlife; Martin Bohl of the Northwest Intertribal Court System; Lawrence Joseph of the Sauk-Suiattle Tribe, Gerald I. James and Bob Davis of the Lummi Indian Nation; James Harp of the Quinault Indian Nation; Dale Griggs and Harry Cooper, Jr. of the Nooksack Tribe, Lee Evenhuis of the Squaxin Island Tribe; John Drotts of the Stillaguamish Tribe; Paul Hage of the Muckleshoot Tribe; Nick Lampsakis of the Point No Point Treaty Council; Brad Sele and Ann Seiter of the Jamestown Klallam Tribe; Lorraine Loomis of the Swinomish Tribe and the Skagit System Cooperative; James Jorgenson of the Hoh Tribe; David Troutt of the Nisqually Tribe; and William Warren, fisheries manager, and Frank Wright Jr. and Harold Harris, fish commissioners from the Puyallup Tribe. My apologies to anyone who has been inadvertently omitted.

Finally, I wish to thank my children, Vali and Mockalee, who have been tolerant of my inattentiveness throughout the duration of this project, and Tuki and Cody, whose interests in fish are heartfelt and whose companionship has been welcome. Most of all, I wish to thank Michael Taylor, who taught me the importance of understanding the place where you live and whose patience, sound advice, and unflagging support and encouragement have sustained me throughout.

Introduction

This book is a theoretical and empirical investigation into the evolution of institutions of self-governance in the area of natural resource management. The theoretical emphasis is on problems of collective action and the evolution of rules and practices centered on the resolution of such practices. The empirical focus is on a regulatory regime in which 20 Pacific Northwest Indian tribes comanage the area's salmon fisheries along with the Washington State Department of Fish and Wildlife and various other federal and international regulatory bodies. This innovative system of joint decision making has been a model for other groups seeking more localized control over resource policy and is of considerable interest to public-policy practitioners as well as scholars interested in issues of natural resource management, institutional design, and participatory democracy.

The book attempts to answer two interrelated questions. First, can user groups effectively manage renewable natural resource systems? Second, do institutions that emerge in settings where individuals and groups are relatively autonomous reflect principles of allocative efficiency and serve to maximize aggregate wealth? If not, what values do they appear to reflect?

Institutions are rules and practices—formal or informal—that structure social interaction. The question of whether institutions tend to evolve in the direction of efficiency, defined as aggregate wealth maximization, is currently being explored and tested in a number of areas. For some years Richard Posner has advanced the argument that the common law evolves in the direction of efficiency or wealth maximization (1977). He has expanded the domain of this claim to law and custom in primitive society (1980) and a variety of modern, nonlegal contexts. Robert Ellickson, another law and economics scholar, has published a study of the content of informal norms among California cattlemen (1991) in which he concludes that such norms are welfare maximizing, although he notes that such a result may obtain only in close-knit groups. A number of studies in economic history have attempted to demonstrate that efficient property rights (these are generally defined as *private* property rights) tend to emerge and evolve in situations of increasing scarcity (Demsetz 1967; Anderson and Leal 1991; Libecap 1989).

Yet clearly efficiency is not always the underlying principle of institutional design, or at least not the only principle. The primary purpose of some institutions seems to be the further enrichment or empowerment of the already rich and powerful or maintenance of the status quo. Conversely, it has been argued that since many institutions serve to redistribute wealth, their primary effect is to increase social cohesion. Without further research into the mechanisms through which efficiency (or some other value) becomes manifest in institutions, it is impossible to adjudicate between these claims. What is needed is work that specifies the microfoundations upon which institutions rest by studying a situation where there is a great deal of innovative institutional change—where real individuals are creating new institutions while weighing the outcomes they are likely to generate in light of issues such as efficiency and equity. This book attempts to contribute to that research program.

One function of many existing institutions appears to be to assist people in coordinating and cooperating with each other for mutual gain. This function is particularly important in situations where individuals face incentives to take actions that, collectively, result in suboptimal outcomes. Collective action problems resulting from a disjuncture between individual and collective rationality appear in nearly all aspects of social, political, and economic life, from team production among workers to negotiations between nation-states, to transactions between firms and consumers, to relations between members of a family. Unsolved collective action problems exist whenever individuals fail to realize possible gains from cooperation. Solving a collective action problem invariably has a distributive aspect since potential solutions distribute costs and benefits differently (Coleman, Heckathorn, and Maser 1989; Coleman 1992). Reaching an agreement on the distribution problem is a necessary condition to solving the larger problem.

Failures to solve collective action problems are particularly apparent in the management of natural resource systems such as fisheries, forests, groundwater aquifers, and the global atmosphere. Although regenerative if used within certain limits, such resource systems are exhaustible if subjected to exploitation beyond a certain carrying capacity. Individuals may face incentives to continue extracting additional resource units beyond the optimal point since the costs of such excess takings are spread across the group, but the benefits go directly to the individual user. Yet if all users do so, the result is overexploitation and perhaps the collapse of the resource system, an outcome no one wants. In the words of the economist, the outcome is inefficient. From an environmentalist's perspective, it may be an ecological disaster.

Institutions are particularly important in situations like this because they can structure incentives in such a way as to guide individuals toward superior outcomes. For many years after Garrett Hardin published his famous article entitled "The Tragedy of the Commons," it was generally believed that the institutions that could alleviate this problem could come about only through the establishment of government ownership and control or through the creation of individual private property rights (G. Hardin 1968). Today, this theory is still believed by many resource policy analysts, economists, and other social scientists. Yet there is growing empirical evidence that suggests that self-governing user communities, which share some form of collective property right over a given resource, can design appropriate efficient institutions for managing small-scale, bounded common-pool resources (Ostrom 1990; McCay and Acheson 1987; McKean 1986; Netting 1981, 1982; Baland and Platteau 1996). From a practical as well as theoretical standpoint, it is extremely important to determine how and when such self-governing regimes can function efficiently. It is particularly important to test their viability with respect to the management of a large, transboundary resource.

This study involves a close examination of a number of small communities who share management of the Pacific Northwest salmon fisheries along with the Washington State Department of Fish and Wildlife, various federal agencies, and international regulatory panels. This unusual management regime came about as the result of a 1974 federal court decision, which ruled that local Indians have a treaty right to catch up to one-half the harvestable salmon in the case area. Initially the decision met with stiff resistance; currently comanagement functions fairly smoothly.

Tribal fisheries are a particularly good place to test competing hypotheses about how efficiency and other values are reflected in institutional design, for several reasons. First, decision making is relatively autonomous. Within a specified regulatory framework, tribes are free to set their own rules regarding fishery management. Second, these institutions are new. Most were either created or have undergone major change in the last 25 years, thus it is still possible to trace their origins and evolution in response to changing conditions. Third, the fishery resource is currently under a great deal of pressure from both intertribal and state-tribal competition, as well as increased crowding between members of particular tribes. Tribes are currently making difficult decisions about how they will manage intertribal allocation as well as whether they will limit entry among their own members. This decision-making process illuminates many of the efficiency-versus-equity questions that this study seeks to answer.

The book is organized as follows. Chapter 1 begins with a discussion of collective action problems. The general discussion is made more specific by applying it to a complex of problems that plague managers of many natural resource systems, problems that are sometimes termed *open access* problems, *common-pool* problems, or *commons* problems. Next, I evaluate various institutional responses that have been suggested by economists, public-policy analysts, and other social scientists. The chapter closes with a brief overview of the Pacific Northwest salmon fishery and the particular problems it raises with respect to the theoretical material.

Chapter 2 takes a step backward in time to examine the institutions used by aboriginal people in organizing themselves in order to utilize a highly productive yet temporally variable resource. In this chapter I explore the notion of efficiency in a premarket setting. I conclude that in these tribal societies, efficiency-enhancing institutions were achievable because they existed in the context of a network of redistributive institutions.

Chapter 3 gives a brief sketch of the development of the fishery from the time of the treaties in the mid-nineteenth century, through the cannery era up to the period of heavy utilization and severe overcrowding of the mid- to late twentieth century. I analyze what is, for the purposes of this study, one of the most important events of the recent period—the federal district court decision that divided the fish between treaty and nontreaty fishermen and sharply limited the state's role in regulating the Indian fishery. One objective of this chapter is to give the reader a road map to what is an enormously complicated management and planning process involving numerous parties whose interests alternately conflict and converge, who are attempting to manage a valuable resource with fairly exacting biological requirements while at the same time working within the legal principles laid out by the court.

Over the years, a dense web of formal and informal agreements has grown up between the parties, which helps organize the way various management tasks are carried out and, most importantly, structure the conflict and competition that invariably accompany allocation of a scarce resource. These institutions—formal and informal, written and unwritten—are the focus of chapters 4, 5, and 6. Chapter 4 looks at relations between the tribes and state, federal, and international regulatory bodies. Chapter 5 looks at intertribal management issues, particularly the increasingly thorny problems of intertribal allocation. Chapter 6 considers the internal decision-making processes used by different tribes in attempting to balance conservation needs with equity and efficiency.

Each chapter presents a different set of problems, yet the opportunities and strategies available at one level are influenced by and in turn influence the strategies and opportunities available at another. Each major interaction is in effect a "nested game" in which negotiating parties must continually reassess which of their current adversaries are likely to be potential allies on some issue in the future (Tsebelis 1990).

The final chapter attempts to pull together these disparate threads and draw from this case some lessons that are applicable more generally. This case sheds light on how people choose to balance efficiency with other values and how conservation and the future value of a resource are weighed against the present employment needs of group members. The findings give rise to conclusions about the potential for local use-group management of natural resources, the appropriate division of labor among regulatory agencies, and the prospects for social cooperation more generally.

In addition to whatever theoretical interest this case may hold, the Pacific Northwest salmon fisheries are important in their own right. While any resource system, however small, is important to those who depend on it, Pacific salmon occupy a unique place in the region's history and identity. Badly managed in the past, and currently beset with competition from other users of water resources, the salmon fishery continues to employ several thousand commercial fishermen and provide recreation to more than a million sport fishermen (Washington State Department of Fish and Wildlife 1995). In 1991 and 1992, four wild salmon stocks from the neighboring Columbia River system were listed under the federal Endangered Species Act. In 1994, for the first time in its history, the federal agency responsible for managing ocean fisheries shut down nearly all ocean salmon fishing in Washington and Oregon out of concern for some critically low wild salmon stocks. Although ultimately their fate is likely to be determined by decisions regarding land use, residential development, logging practices, and hydroelectric energy use, the vulnerability of many stocks of wild salmon drive home the importance of well-designed fishery management institutions.

CHAPTER 1

Social Cooperation and the Problem of Collective Action

How individuals or groups succeed—and fail—in cooperating with each other constitutes a large part of the study of politics. Obstacles to social cooperation spring from a variety of sources, and many of them will not receive a full treatment here. The primary focus of this study is on that subset of barriers to social cooperation termed *collective action problems* and on the evolution of institutions designed to combat such problems. Even more specifically, it concerns problems that arise in the management of natural resource systems and on the institutions with which individuals have tried to regulate their use of such systems.

The failure of many current institutional arrangements to manage natural resource systems sustainably is apparent the world over. In some cases, failure comes about through the vulnerability of traditional institutions to threats posed by the presence of new economic opportunities or from population pressures. In others, where management is ostensibly under state control, there are frequently problems with efficient implementation and enforcement and with questions of equity. *Comanagement* is a term given to governance systems that combine state control with local, decentralized decision making and accountability and which, ideally, combine the strengths and mitigate the weaknesses of each. In addition to their practical significance, the creation and maintenance of comanagement systems illuminate several of the central puzzles that lie at the heart of institutional design. For example, how do social actors with different skills and both shared and competing interests create structures that allow them to work together productively? How are mechanisms for credible commitment and for monitoring and enforcement established and maintained? A more specific set of questions arises in the context of the management of natural resource systems. Does giving greater autonomy to local users of a resource system elicit increased cooperation and consent with regulatory controls, or does it create conflicts of interest that make such systems more vulnerable to overexploitation? And since such comanagement regimes often emerge from a history of mutual distrust and resistance, how do the parties create an environment where trust may develop and it is no longer necessary to invest heavily in safeguards against opportunistic behavior?

The chapter begins with a discussion of the general problem of collective action and the role institutions play in helping resolve such problems. Next, it focuses on renewable resources and the range of institutional arrangements that has been proposed to bring about successful management of these resource systems. Finally, it sets out what I think this study, an analysis of what is one of the oldest and most sophisticated comanagement regimes in existence, can contribute to that debate and the larger subjects of social cooperation and the emergence and maintenance of institutions.

The Problem of Collective Action

Collective action problems can be defined as situations where actions that are rational from an individual standpoint result in outcomes that are collectively suboptimal or irrational (Taylor 1987, R. Hardin 1982). Situations in which individual rationality and group rationality are at odds are extremely common. One widely discussed example of collective action problems is the provision of public goods. The paradoxical logic behind this conflict between individual and collective rationality is familiar to most social scientists. If the costs of contributing to a public good are borne privately while the benefits are shared throughout the group regardless of whether particular individuals have contributed, there is an incentive to "free ride" on the efforts of others. As long as this incentive exists (and there are no countering incentives), there is a presumption that the public good will be provided suboptimally, if at all (Olson 1965; R. Hardin 1982).

The public good may be an organization, as in Olson's original formulation, or it may be a rule or set of institutional arrangements or governance structures. The common element is that such goods involve individual contributions to a good that is public, that is, a good or service that is to some extent nonexcludable and indivisible. Analytically, it makes no difference whether such contributions involve time, money, or goods, or whether they result from forgoing opportunities, although in practical terms such differences may affect the ease or difficulty of monitoring or enforcing agreements intended to resolve such problems.

Conservation of Natural Resource Systems

Most environmental problems involve resource systems that are to some extent nonexcludable, and many of them are currently badly degraded as a result of overexploitation. Overfishing, overgrazing, or use of the global atmosphere as a dumping site may occur simply because individuals believe that it is in their best interests to use a resource heavily in the present even if that means using it up, or because they believe the costs of certain actions can be passed on to another party. The near destruction of the whale fishery at the end of the nineteenth century may have been an example of the first situation, and the problem of American industries dumping airborne pollution on Canada is an instance of the second, if the collectivity is defined as consisting of American industries. Neither of these situations would constitute collective action problems in the sense that is intended here. Collective action problems exist only if people actually would have preferred to act differently but were, in effect, trapped by the interactive effects of their relations with others.

Like public goods, natural resource systems are nonexcludable, or at least exclusion is costly to impose. Unlike public goods, however, the products of a resource system are divisible and can be brought under sole ownership by capture. Such goods are sometimes called *common-pool resources* or *common property resources* (CPRs). In the case of public goods provision, the collective action problem results in underprovision; in the case of CPRs, the result can be overexploitation and overcapitalization as individuals compete for units of a "free" resource.

For example, if there are no barriers to my taking as many fish from a lake as I like, I will continue to do so until the marginal cost of taking an additional fish is just equal to the marginal benefit to me. As early models in fisheries economics demonstrated, when the resource stock is shared, this point is not reached until the marginal cost to each new fisherman is equal to the average benefit or average product; consequently fishermen will continue to enter the fishery until the average product is zero (Gordon 1954). More recent economic models show that fishermen are likely to stop entering the fishery somewhere before this point because of the private costs incurred by each fisherman (Dasgupta 1982), but the basic point remains the same—open access to resource stocks results in inefficiency.

For regenerative resources, the problem is compounded by the fact that the subtraction of resource units has effects on resource stocks. Once the point of maximum sustainable yield has been reached, the future viability of the system may be jeopardized by additional harvesting. In this case, the full costs of an action include not only its immediate costs but also its effects on future benefits. But since the marginal benefits of taking an additional fish (or of inexpensively disposing of an extra ton of pollutants) go entirely to the individual, while the costs are spread throughout the group, the individual's calculation will not reflect the full costs and benefits of the action being taken, at least not if extrarational motivations are ruled out. The overall result of these two dimensions of inefficiency is that there will be too many fishermen with too much gear chasing smaller and fewer fish.

This unfortunate result is not confined to fisheries, although fisheries and wildlife present particularly difficult problems because they involve migratory resources. The more general point is that when private and social costs diverge, inefficient outcomes result. If there are no barriers to an individual or a firm or a nation exporting its pollution by dumping it in the river or sending it up in the air to be carried away by prevailing winds, then that activity will, in effect, receive a subsidy at the expense of the larger collectivity. Successful management is possible with the creation of institutions that bring private costs in line with social costs, but since such institutions are themselves public goods, their creation and maintenance constitute problems in their own right.

In either of these categories of situations, individuals have incentives to free ride on the efforts of others. A likely result is that everyone ends up at a less-preferred point than if each had adopted a different strategy.

Exchange and Joint Production

It is less common to hear problems of exchange and joint production discussed in these terms, yet problems of contracting and collaboration between regulatory agencies, between firms, and with respect to relations among coworkers or between employees and employers have analogous structures. The same can be said for other sorts of organizations and any project that requires teamwork. Consider the problems faced by a group of workers whose job performance ratings rest on the group's output. Each member has an incentive to work at a fairly leisurely pace since expending large amounts of energy on a task will only raise the group's output by a relatively small amount. When everyone shirks, output drops and so may salaries. Everyone would rather that everyone worked harder, but no one will chose to do so unless each individual can be assured that others will also.[1] Again, the most-preferred outcome is individually inaccessible.

Relations between workers and owners are overshadowed by the same problem. Each stands to gain by exchanging rights to the assets under their control—for workers, their own labor power, and for owners, the resources they will expend in paying workers and in furnishing physical capital—because joint production allows for greater return on those

---

1. Many production processes are characterized by interdependency, which makes it impossible (or prohibitively costly) to separate each participant's contribution and thus creates the potential for shirking (Alchian and Demsetz 1972).

assets than alternative uses do. We can assume that both sides prefer mutual cooperation to mutual defection. Yet each side is haunted by, on the one hand, the temptation to shirk at the other's expense, and on the other, the fear that the same will be done to them. Either party would contribute more if they could be sure that the other side was also contributing and if they were satisfied with their share of the surplus that results from their collaboration.

The latter point introduces another problem. A given surplus can go either to the owners (shareholders or executives) in the form of profits or to the workers in the form of increased wages or benefits. Stakeholders in a natural resource system or regulatory agencies with overlapping jurisdictions may face a similarly uncertain situation with respect to who will reap the benefits of a more productive resource system or more efficient management regime. An inability to negotiate an agreement over each side's share will preclude a resolution of the shirking problem. An additional bargaining problem is that individual workers, unless they possess unique skills, are in a fairly weak bargaining position relative to owners. The same logic applies when small organizations or organizations with few exceptional assets attempt to bargain with a much larger and more powerful political entity. Joining together and bargaining collectively strengthens the position of workers or organizations, although overcoming collective action problems generates its own costs, such as the need to pay union officials or create umbrella organizations to represent them, which in turn creates the need to monitor an agent's performance to make sure the agent is fully representing their interests.

Firms, government agencies, and other organizations face similar problems of joint production when they contemplate entering into long-term contracts with others (Williamson 1975, 1985). The benefits of specialization make such collaborative efforts attractive, but such relationships, particularly if they involve specialized investments, carry inherent risks. With firms, the danger is that once a supplier has made investments specific to a particular contract or relationship, it will be vulnerable to efforts by the buyer to lower the agreed-upon price, since there are unlikely to be competing bids. In the case of regulatory agencies, a cooperative outcome would be one in which each agency focused its efforts on activities in which it has a comparative advantage and resisted the temptation to use its particular skills opportunistically. Yet mutual mistrust often results in each side duplicating the efforts of the other or in either side failing to comply with regulations that rest on information gathered by the other. With any exchange—between firms and bureaucracies and between firms and customers or workers—not all attributes of the information or item being exchanged are immediately obvious, and sellers will have both incentives and opportunities to conceal their true value. The result may be fewer long-term contracts or a less-integrated relationship than either side would have preferred—a deadweight loss.

In each of the disparate situations sketched, the problem is that individuals face structural incentives to adopt strategies that lead to outcomes that are collectively suboptimal. What are the underlying conditions that lead to such social dilemmas?

Externalities and Asymmetric Information

Externalities are aspects of a transaction that are not directly accounted for within the transaction itself. They arise in part because few goods or services are wholly divisible and excludable. Most goods are bundles of attributes, some of which are divisible and excludable, some of which are nonexcludable and indivisible. The use to which a good is put will partially determine how susceptible it is to externality problems. For example, a forest can be looked upon alternately as a quantity of standing timber that can be transformed into so many feet of lumber, a habitat for various flora and fauna, a recreational area for hikers or off-road vehicle users, a scientific laboratory for zoologists or botanists, or a source of satisfaction to a given proportion of the population whose lives are enriched by the mere fact that this forest exists. Different goods or different uses for the same good represent a wide range along the dimensions of divisibility and excludability. The extent to which some uses generate public goods will, ceteris paribus, result in their underprovision.

In any exchange, there are asymmetries in the information available to the parties or in the costs of acquiring such information.[2] Workers know more about their own capacities and day-to-day expenditures of effort than do their employers; owners know more about the productive capacities of the assets they control; regulatory agencies know more about the different resources and skills they contribute to collaborative endeavors; and citizens are at a disadvantage in determining whether government representatives are truly representing their interests. Generally, it is difficult and costly for parties without such intimate knowledge to acquire it.

One result of asymmetric information is that people will be dissuaded

---

2. The problem of asymmetric information would not loom so large were it not for variability in the attributes of things normally classified as the same. Such variability creates measurement costs. See Barzel 1982; 1989 for a discussion of the importance of measurement costs and the multiplicity of institutions and practices that have evolved to mitigate those costs.

from entering into relationships that would make them better off.[3] That is, of course, an inefficient outcome. Typically, the party with more information will expend resources in trying to persuade the less-informed party that she or he is in fact acting without guile. For example, elected officials spend a great deal of their own and their staff's time "advertising" their accomplishments (Mayhew 1974). While a small fraction of these activities convey useful information, much of it results in deadweight losses that are in large part attributable to the problem of asymmetric information and the failure to solve collective action problems.

Transaction Costs

Despite the ubiquity of externalities and situations of asymmetric information, in practice, many collective action problems are solved. Neither individuals nor companies normally dump wastes directly into nearby waterways, or if they do, they are liable to be fined. Not all regenerative resource systems are in a state of collapse, and some firms maintain a high level of productivity. A whole range of institutions have been created to respond to problems of collective action. Before turning to these, it is important to specify more clearly what an institution must do to solve the problem.

Externalities and asymmetric information give rise to collective action problems because they generate costs. Successful resolution of collective action problems involves expending resources on three kinds of costs: (1) search costs, (2) bargaining costs, and (3) monitoring and enforcement costs (Dahlman 1979). Collectively, these are called *transaction costs,* and any durable solution to the problems that are present in the situations described earlier must meet these costs.

Search costs include defining the causes and scope of the problem and the range of possible solutions, locating potential partners or parties to an exchange or cooperative effort, and establishing what contribution they are capable of making as well as gathering information about their preferences and reputations for reliability. Bargaining costs involve negotiating over various possible solutions, each of which can be expected to differ in terms of the distribution of returns to the parties. The presence of a multitude of alternatives that could solve a given dilemma is one of the primary obstacles to efficiency (Coleman, Heckathorn, and Maser 1989; Libecap 1989). If bargaining problems are severe and solving them likely to be very

---

3. This point was first made by Akerlof (1970). There is now an extensive literature on the problems of moral hazard and adverse selection.

costly, there may be no resolution to the larger problem. Finally, monitoring and enforcement are ongoing tasks, and the ease or difficulty of accomplishing them will vary depending on the extent to which information is asymmetric, the incentives each side has to continue the relationship, the legal regime, and even the available technology. Although these transaction costs are listed chronologically, it is unlikely that a collective action problem will be resolved by moving from one stage to another. Potential cooperators can be expected to anticipate the probable costs of any of these stages almost immediately, and sufficiently high costs at any stage will preclude the process before it has really begun. Distributive issues in particular are likely to strongly influence the type of solution or even whether there will be a solution (Knight 1992).

Understanding transaction costs is key to understanding the structure of institutions. Both were virtually ignored in traditional economic models. The recent emphasis on transaction costs draws heavily on two articles by economist Ronald Coase. In "The Problem of Social Cost," Coase argues that in a world of zero transaction costs, the initial distribution of property rights is irrelevant because private bargaining will result in socially optimal outcomes (Coase 1960). Drawing exactly the wrong implication, some economists interpreted this argument as evidence for the superiority of voluntary exchange relative to government intervention. That was ironic, since the real significance of Coase's work was to highlight the importance and omnipresence of transaction costs. In an earlier article, Coase asked why firms exist when individuals could conduct all their exchanges through the market. By focusing attention on the costs of market exchange and consequent development of hierarchical institutions such as the firm, Coase again highlighted the importance of transaction costs and institutions (Coase 1937).

A considerable body of literature has developed that attempts to explain the existence of various institutions in terms of their role in mitigating transaction costs and deadweight losses. The new institutionalism began among economists who were dissatisfied with the limitations of the Walsarian model of full information and costless exchanges. Since then, a fair number of social scientists from other disciplines have used the transaction-cost approach to explain a broad range of political phenomena.[4] Transaction costs have been used to explain long-term institutional change (North 1981), the choice of tax policies by rulers in a variety of historical settings (Levi 1988), the timing of the privatization of rangeland in the American West (Anderson and Hill 1975), norms for settling dis-

---

4. For a critique of the wholesale importation of the transaction-cost approach to the study of bureaucracies, see Moe 1984.

putes and sharing fence-building expenses among ranchers in northern California (Ellickson 1991), division rules among whalers (Ellickson 1989), the structure of farmland rental contracts (Allen and Lueck 1992; Cheung 1970; Barzel 1989), and the emergence of property rights in a variety of historical settings including anarchic mining camps in mid-nineteenth-century America (Umbeck 1981) and the hunting territories of various aboriginal people of North America during the early contact period (Demsetz 1967).

In the study of American political institutions, the transaction-cost approach has been utilized to explain the durability of policy bargains among legislators (Weingast and Marshall 1988), the committee system and its function in the designation of property rights over particular policy areas (Shepsle and Weingast 1981), and the style of congressional over-sight of bureaucracies (Weingast and Moran 1983; McCubbins and Schwartz 1984).This by no means exhaustive list gives some indications of where this approach has been productively employed. In what follows, I will apply the transaction-cost approach to the problem of the management of natural resource systems, particularly fisheries.

Collective Action and the Management of Natural Resource Systems

What Is Successful Management?

Definitions of what constitutes success in natural resource management generally include both efficiency and equity. Under a standard efficiency criterion, a successfully managed resource system would be one that is being utilized at maximum sustainable yield, that is, the maximum level of harvest that is consistent with a similar level of use in the future.[5] An efficient set of institutions would be those that encourage individuals to employ inputs—human effort and skill as well as physical assets such as technology and natural resources—in their most productive use, defined as the use that is likely to yield the greatest utility to a given population.[6] An

---

5. This criterion assumes that the rate of regeneration and discount rate of the owner(s) are not inconsistent with the preservation of the resource system. While that seems to be a reasonable assumption in most cases and is the one that will be used throughout this study, there are certain cases where these assumptions would not hold. For example, C. W. Clark (1977) argues that the regeneration rate of whales is so slow that it was economically rational for users to almost completely decimate the whale population. That was not, then, a "commons" problem, if the collectivity is defined as consisting solely of whalers.

6. Obviously, this relationship becomes difficult to specify if there is significant uncertainty about or variability between different populations with respect to what represents utility.

efficient set of institutions will not necessarily result in the highest levels of output—there may be random or unpredictable events that affect output, or individuals may be mistaken in their beliefs. Efficient institutions allow individuals to do the best they can, given limited information.

Equity, particularly redistributional equity, is often considered to be in conflict with efficiency (Okun 1975). In most public-policy texts, the policymaker's task is seen as one of balancing a number of competing values, but most centrally those of efficiency and redistributional equity. In this study, it will be argued that once the considerable transaction costs associated with solving the collective action problems are taken into account, this apparent opposition begins to look overstated. Only in an idealized world of zero transaction costs, where there is perfect information and property rights are completely specified, is it possible to characterize as efficient institutions that do not consider distributional equity. In the real world, equity and other social values significantly affect the efficiency of institutions because they alter the transaction costs associated with specifying and enforcing them.

The Privatization Prescription

Problems with the management of common-pool resources have not lacked policy prescriptions. Traditionally, economists have tended to focus on the benefits of establishing private property rights. The expectation is that through the establishment of private property rights, individual and social costs will be brought into accord and the inefficiencies of resource use under open access will disappear. Members of the so-called property rights school have sought to demonstrate empirically that in conditions of increasing scarcity, prevailing institutional arrangements will evolve in the direction of more strictly defined private property rights (Demsetz 1967). While the simplicity and elegance of the privatization solution are initially compelling, at least if normative considerations such as equity are set aside, much of the attraction fades once transaction costs are taken into account. For example, distributive issues affect perceptions of equity, which in turn affect the costs associated with implementation and enforcement.

Advocates of privatization generally fail to consider the transaction costs associated with creating and maintaining a private property regime. Such costs include initial outlays, both public and private, of measuring and evaluating a resource system and adjudicating distributional claims. Ongoing public costs include policing and support from the legal system. Costs borne privately may include the initial costs of negotiating, lobbying government, and so on that are involved in establishing rights, and the costs of policing and defending one's property.

Other costs are difficult to quantify but nonetheless significant. It is rare for governments or individuals to pay the full costs of enforcing a rule or right. To do so would be prohibitively expensive. Much enforcement is provided though decentralized means, through self-sanctioning or social controls. Successful institutions are those that can in effect be piggybacked onto preexisting systems of social control. The extent to which people are willing to pay the costs of instituting privatization will vary according to the expectations and shared beliefs of a particular society and the distributional effects of the change. This principle will be true even if the change could generate sufficient surplus such that "winners" could compensate "losers" and still be better off, since the high transaction costs of such compensatory measures will cause potential losers to doubt that they will occur. They are thus likely to attempt to block such a change.

Resource systems have different characteristics, which affect the cost and feasibility of privatization. A resource system with few indivisibilities, such as some rangelands or pastures, can be converted to units of private property fairly easily. The fact that it is feasible does not mean that rational individuals would chose to do so. If there are economies of scale in production, there may be good economic reasons not to privatize, for exactly the same reasons that many economic exchanges are more expeditiously performed within a firm, rather than through the market. This idea is demonstrated nicely in Carl Dahlman's investigation into the open field system (1980). By utilizing the open field system, peasants were able to combine institutions of common property ownership over grazing areas, which allowed them to take advantage of economies of scale, with private property in arable land, where the most efficient unit of production was the individual family. For resources whose utilization requires team production, the same sort of reasoning applies. Establishing private property rights and then exchanging them through the market is sometimes too costly, relative to alternative arrangements.[7]

For some sorts of resource systems, it is hard to imagine how privatization would be possible. The global atmosphere would be difficult to privatize, as would the world's oceans. If for no other reason, the cost of monitoring and policing the boundaries of such a resource would be prohibitive. Even where it is possible to divide up a resource base, many resource stocks are composed of mobile or fugitive resources. Various

---

7. This is Coase's explanation for the existence of firms—that hierarchy is, in some cases, a more efficient method of contracting than market exchange (1937).

species of salmon, for example, cover several thousand miles during their life cycles, crossing and recrossing numerous local, state, and international boundaries. A private property right in fish is a hollow claim unless one can exclude others from intercepting them.

Determining when size is or is not a problem partly depends on how a resource system is to be used. A forest, if it is to be used for timber production, can readily be privatized. If, on the other hand, it is to be used for habitat for certain species of wildlife or for hiking trails, fairly large parcels are required and the costs of negotiating separate agreements with individual owners may be prohibitive. Advocates of privatization of public lands often miss the fact that in a world where information is imperfect and transacting is costly, and where resources have characteristics of both public and private goods, individual voluntary exchanges alone will not result in socially optimal outcomes.

State Ownership and Regulation

When privatization is not a workable option, the prescribed policy response has been to create institutions that act as surrogates for private property. Generally that has meant putting the resource in the hands of the state, which then restricts access in some fashion, through limits on inputs or outputs or through the allocation of permits or licenses. With fisheries, for example, limited-entry or license limitations have been the predominant fisheries policy instrument during the last 25 years. Under a limited-entry program, the government determines the number of boats or fishermen necessary to harvest the catch and attempts to limit licenses accordingly under some predetermined distribution rule. In effect, the government creates a type of property right. Once distributed, licenses may be transferable or nontransferable. Most state management regimes would also include time and area closures and gear restrictions, which limit the exercise of such rights.

Assessments of the evidence on limited-entry programs show mixed but generally disappointing results (Townsend 1990). Most limited-entry programs are simply too weak; they allow too many licenses to be issued and the fishery continues to be overfished and overcapitalized. In the most successful cases, either the program was begun in the early stages of the development of the fishery or it was introduced when the fishery was at a trough in a long-term biological cycle and thus had fewer prospective entrants. In fisheries that are already overcrowded, or in situations where entry restrictions are introduced on a piecemeal basis, limited-entry programs have done little to reduce overfishing or unproductive investments (in bigger, faster boats, etc.).

The main problem is the potential for political conflict. Politically, it is difficult to justify limits while the fishery is still uncrowded, and state managers usually wait until overcrowding is blindingly obvious.[8] It is nearly impossible, however, to get broad support among fishermen for any plan that would force some of them out of the fishery. As noted earlier, the fact that there is a plan that would allow winners to compensate losers and still come out ahead does not mean they will do so, and those who would be forced out are well aware of that. The only plan that is likely to receive support from fishermen and their political allies is one that gives licenses to all those currently in the fishery and simply limits new entrants.[9] And if the issue is debated too long, even this potential reduction is undermined as prospective fishermen rush to enter the fishery before licenses are frozen.

The other major difficulty is that simply restricting licenses allows— even encourages—fishermen to overcapitalize on whatever unregulated margins remain. For example, if individuals are limited to one boat per given fishery, boat size and power will increase. If authorities put a lid on boat size, fishermen will invest in larger engines or other technologies to enhance their harvesting capabilities. The peculiar and often unsafe design of boats in some fisheries is traceable to the incentives created by limits on boat size. The more complex a fishery is in terms of species variety and number of gear types, the more margins there are and the easier it will be for fishermen to subvert the purpose of whatever regulations are placed on them by management authorities.

All state regulatory regimes use some sort of gear restrictions and time and area closures. Where a limited-entry system is very weak, they may be the only effective way of protecting the resource. During even a short opening, a large fleet can have a devastating impact on the portion of a run that is present during that time period, sometimes threatening to alter the genetic composition of future runs. Fisheries biologists agree that spreading the catch over the entire period in which the fish are expected to be present in an area is sound conservation practice. Managers have responded by instituting shorter openings and more restrictions on gear in order to make each fishing unit less efficient. The result is that boats are idled for much of the time and the economic potential of each unit is delib-

---

8. Recent appraisals of the performance of the eight regional fishery management councils operating under the Magnuson Fishery Conservation and Management Act highlight the salience of this issue. See Shelley, Atkinson, Dorsey, and Brooks (1996).

9. Drawing on their research on the Gulf of Mexico shrimping industry, Johnson and Libecap (1982) attribute such failures to arrive at efficient institutions to high contracting costs that exist because fishermen are heterogeneous, at least with respect to skill, and are thus affected differently by various solutions to the problems of overcrowding and overcapitalization.

erately reduced. The resistance that creates among fishermen can make regulations difficult to enforce.

Output quotas are another means of limiting access to a fishery. Rather than limiting boat size or restricting gear, the state simply determines the appropriate level of harvest and then divides that amount into individual quotas. Such quotas can be transferable or nontransferable. Political conflicts are likely concerning the appropriate criteria for the initial allocation and with respect to ongoing issues of concentration within the industry. While the number of margins a regulatory agency must monitor and enforce is decreased with an individual quota system, incentives to cheat by fishing over the allowable quota are still present. Enforcement costs can in large part determine whether an individual quota system is feasible (Huppert interview 1992). In fisheries with relatively few producers and a small number of landing ports that can be easily monitored by authorities (the Pacific halibut fishery is a good example), this regime can work well. For the Pacific salmon fisheries, however, where there are many fishermen and fishermen can land their catch almost anywhere, the enforcement and administrative costs would be very high and there is little serious consideration of it.

Because it is difficult to observe or monitor fishermen's compliance with regulations, enforcement costs are potentially very high under state management. State managers must depend in large part on the voluntary cooperation of individual fishermen or on informal social sanctioning practiced by fishermen themselves. In situations where there are hostile or mutually distrustful relations between fishermen and state managers, "crises of consent" have been the result (Pinkerton 1989, 23). Whether or not such crises entail a wholesale paralysis of regulatory authority depends on the depth of mistrust, the economic incentives that drive people to cheat, and the amount of resources the state is willing to commit to monitoring and enforcement.

The difficulties that states have had in managing fisheries highlight the transaction costs that any management system must meet in regulating fisheries. They include:

Data collection and analysis.   Prior to entering the politically charged bargaining phase of deciding who is entitled to licenses or individual quotas or making decisions concerning allocation between different gear types, managers must first gather and analyze data about the status of the resource. Even in relatively simple cases, it is a time-consuming and expensive process. For complex fisheries with multiple stocks in areas where habitat is deteriorating due to adverse impacts from logging, agriculture, or the development of hydroelectric power, the task of modeling run sizes and determining the optimal rate of harvest is vastly more complicated.

Efforts to determine stock size, necessary escapement ratios, and interaction effects between stocks are essential initial steps for successful fisheries management. They require large amounts of biological information that is costly to acquire (Huppert 1992). Furthermore, such information may be highly localized due to the great variety of microclimates within a given area.

Development of a management plan. This entails determining what combination of gear requirements, time and area closures, licensing schemes, or quotas will result in the optimum sustainable yield for the targeted stock(s). To the extent that there are many stocks that overlap or whose biological requirements differ, multiple gear types, or groups of fishermen who are separated geographically but who fish on the same stocks, the difficulty and costliness of this task will increase. With or without explicit decisions regarding allocation, the effect of management decisions will be to allocate fish to one or another user group.

Administration, monitoring and enforcement. Without adequate monitoring and enforcement, no plan will be successful. The potential costs of this aspect of management will frequently influence the choice of policy instruments such as quotas, limited entry, and time, place, and gear restrictions.

Anyone who doubts that such costs are significant should consider a study done by two fisheries economists on the transaction costs of managing fisheries conducted in the 3 to 200 mile Exclusive Economic Zone established by the United States in 1977. They conclude that the United States spent approximately $200 million annually on data collection, administration, and research and an additional $100 million on enforcement. They estimate the total economic benefits from this fishery at between $200 million and $500 million annually (Andersen and Sutinen 1985, 388). The study is unusual; most work on fisheries management policies assumes away transaction costs. This omission has seriously compromised the ability of state managers to design and implement sound management plans.

Local User-Group Solutions

The view that common-pool resources must be *either* privatized, in which case owners are expected to internalize the costs of their actions, *or* owned and managed by the state, which is expected to control externalities through the use of positive and negative incentives, has not gone unchallenged. A disparate group of anthropologists, sociologists, and political scientists point to a large number of cases where local groups have coexisted prosperously with the natural environment for a very long time without the benefit of either centralized political authority or wholesale privatization. While there have been "tragedies" of the sort envisioned by Garrett Hardin (1968), that has not been the rule (see McCay and Acheson 1987; McKean 1986; Netting 1981; Baland and Platteau 1996; and Ostrom 1990 for just a few of the many examples of successful common-pool resource management; see Cordell 1989 and Pinkerton 1989 for examples of successful artisanal fisheries management systems).

Nor has communal ownership been simply a way station between open access and privatization, as some economists might suggest. The coexistence of both private and common property within the same societies, often within the same broad category of economic activity, plus the fact that some societies regularly shift back and forth from private to common-property rules over the same resource, suggests that common-property institutions can come about through the choices of individuals who wish to facilitate an efficient resource utilization strategy.

Much of the work that has been done in this area is based on case studies of local user-group management of a particular common-pool resource. These cases include irrigation systems, mountain pastures, fisheries, and forests. Some trace their roots back a thousand years or more; others are relatively new. Many are currently undergoing great strain under the pressures of growing populations and economic change. Their existence, both in the past and in the present, presents a puzzle: how is it that these resource systems have escaped overexploitation and degradation when there is no state presence to control access to them?

First, it is important to distinguish common-property regimes from situations of open access. Common property is shared property, and co-owners have the same exclusionary rights with respect to outsiders as private property owners do. Open access refers to a situation in which there is no property (Ciriacy-Wantrup and Bishop 1975), and we might expect that overexploitation and overcapitalization are a likely result in situations where there is both scarcity and open access.[10] Once a resource system becomes the shared property of members of a group, however, there are benefits to be had for using the resource system at some optimal level. By creating rules to govern usage, co-owners could share those benefits. There is considerable evidence that such regimes do contain carefully specified

10. See Feeny et al. 1990 for an appraisal of the prospects of successful regulation under open access, state management, and local control. See Stevenson 1991 for a comparison of the efficiency of private property and communal property regimes in Swiss Alpen meadows.

access rules and systems for monitoring and enforcing compliance (Ostrom 1990). Creating rules, monitoring compliance, and enforcing property rights are all costly activities, and individuals have incentives to free ride on the efforts of others. How do groups such as this solve the collective action problems involved in providing themselves with institutions?

At least part of the answer is suggested by formal and experimental work in game theory. Work on the repeated Prisoner's Dilemma game demonstrates that conditional cooperation, in which one party begins by cooperating and then continues to cooperate as long as the other party, or a given subset of the group, also cooperates, can be a rational strategy under certain circumstances (Taylor 1976, 1987; Axelrod 1981; Ostrom, Gardner, and Walker 1994). Iteration, which most would agree is a more realistic approximation of real-life choice situations, is a necessary condition for cooperation, but it is not sufficient. By introducing considerations of the future, iteration can make it more likely that individuals will find it rational to cooperate, although not if individuals discount future benefits highly. If a particular issue is linked with other issues where the participants also share an interest, there will be more opportunities for monitoring and sanctioning, and the value of cooperation in one game may increase because of ripple effects in other spheres of activity. Work done by game theorists also suggests that communication makes it more likely that players will conditionally cooperate and that individuals in small groups are more likely to cooperate (Ostrom, Gardner, and Walker 1994).

The conditions that make conditional cooperation a rational strategy—iteration, low discount rates, and linkage—are approximated in the close-knit communities where many of these successfully managed resource systems are found (Taylor 1982). Michael Taylor has made the more general argument that to the extent a collectivity is a community, its members will be able to solve collective action problems (of all sorts) endogenously, that is, with little or no help from a state. The defining features of community are shared beliefs, stable and multifaceted relations, and rough equality (Taylor 1982). A recent attempt to explore this idea in the context of common-pool resource management gives tentative support to the hypothesis. In situations where these group characteristics are weak, we find such institutions either compromised or nonexistent; in situations where community is strong, we find robust institutions and successfully managed CPRs (Singleton and Taylor 1992).

Roughly the same argument can be made in terms of transaction costs. Certain characteristics of groups will lower the transaction costs that must be met in solving collective action problems. If relations between members are multifaceted, such linkages will give parties additional assurances that they can retaliate against those who defect, as well as additional reasons to cooperate, which will lower the costs of negotiating any particular agreement. The costs of gathering information about the preferences, beliefs, and reputations for trustworthiness of others will be substantially less for members of a community than for a state agency. And to the extent that the user group is homogeneous, the costs of bargaining over solutions will be lowered.

Community management is not a panacea for all the ills plaguing common-pool resource management, however. Even strong communities may have high discount rates, which lead them to overexploit a resource system. In addition, a significant component of the value of many natural resource systems is the public goods they produce. If local communities can obtain income only for the private goods they harvest from the resource system, their utilization patterns may be unsustainably and inefficiently high relative to the full value to the resource. If a local community lacks incentives to manage a resource system sustainably, granting local autonomy may result in a loss to the larger collectivity.

Monitoring and enforcement generate costs for local communities, just as they do for states. In community-based regimes, community members bear a large share of the burden of monitoring and enforcement. It can be a relatively inexpensive system of social control since members can observe the behavior of others fairly effortlessly as they go about their daily lives. Gossip and social disapproval are very effective sanctions in a close-knit community, but they also involve personal cost, uncertainty, and risk. Where pressures to overharvest are great, community controls may be inadequate. Where some level of trust has been established for state regulatory personnel, preexisting community networks can be productively combined with state regulatory power.

Some transaction costs may be relatively low for local user groups simply by virtue of their proximity to the resource system. For example, collecting the data necessary for managing many common-pool resources is costly for state managers but may be readily and inexpensively available to members of a local user group. On the other hand, a resource such as salmon may migrate across large distances, making it difficult for local groups to fully interpret the data they collect or to implement appropriate policies that may extend beyond their jurisdiction. A state agency can be extremely helpful in coordinating the actions of local groups and facilitating agreements between them. States have interests of their own, however, and some of them may involve furthering the interests of one group at the expense of another or some other interest at the expense of the long-term productivity of the resource.

Goals of This Study

Much of the early work on local management of natural resource systems was empirically rich and theoretically highly eclectic, with contributors united primarily through their opposition to the "tragedy of the commons" metaphor and in many cases by a shared distrust of the use of economic models and rational actor models. Today that is no longer true, and there are now a number of theoretically sophisticated typologies, frameworks, and "institutional design principles" that can be used to extract and distill generalizable conclusions from the empirical material.[11] Case studies of small-scale, local user-group management remain a large part of the literature, however, and generally the cases reported on continue to come from rural areas of developing countries.

This study also concerns itself with local management of a CPR, but it is distinct in several respects. First, unlike most studies of CPRs, the Pacific Northwest salmon fisheries are large: the wholesale value of salmon caught in Washington state was nearly $53 million in 1993; the combined number of sport and commercial fishermen in recent years has been well over a million (Washington State Department of Fish and Wildlife 1995, 1996).[12] Since Pacific salmon migrate across thousands of miles and more than a dozen political jurisdictions, the boundaries of this resource system are extensive. In addition, the fishery is exceedingly complex—biologically as well as legally. Biologically sound management decisions must take into consideration the often incompatible needs of the various species and multiple stocks within each species. Decisions that have consequences for allocation, which most do, must weigh the preferences of various treaty and nontreaty user groups, most of which are well organized and capable of exerting great pressure at the level of the state legislature and beyond.

Second, this is a study of a natural resource managed under a hybrid management system. The fishery is neither entirely state managed nor entirely under the control of local communities. Sometimes called *systems of comanagement,* a few such hybrids have been described elsewhere (Pinkerton 1989, Baland and Platteau 1996), but most have been in existence for too short a time period for meaningful conclusions to be drawn concerning their viability. The tribal-state comanagement system in Washington state is arguably the most sophisticated, fully developed system of

---

11. For a sampling of some of the best work of the latter type, see Ostrom 1990; Baland and Platteau 1996; Hanna, Folke, and Maler 1996.

12. Since decisions made by managers of this system also affect other fisheries and, indirectly, a variety of other land management decisions, the real economic effects of their decisions might be seen as several times these amounts.

its kind. At a time when few areas are untouched by the power of states and where previously successful institutions of locally managed commons are being destabilized by increasing heterogeneity among members, population pressures, and exposure to markets, this case offers an opportunity to think about the comparative advantages of centralized versus decentralized management structures and the appropriate division of labor between them.

This study tries to walk the fine line between theory and empirical material. While neoinstitutional or transaction-cost economics has gone a long way toward addressing the flaws in traditional economic models, there has been less work that applies such theory to actual cases. Moreover, the effects of political considerations such as distributional conflict are sometimes absent from such models.[13] This study attempts to clarify how a set of institutions for managing a resource system has actually emerged and evolved, and how its emergence and evolution have been shaped by attempts to resolve the collective action problems that are endemic in such systems. In the process, it tries to be somewhat more careful in specifying what is meant by success. Although most of the cultural anthropologists who study CPRs probably have a better intuitive grasp of the effects that distributional conflict and culture might have on transaction costs and social cooperation, they often pay little attention to the question of efficiency. What is frequently used as a measure of success is whether or not there is an evident pattern of overexploitation. Yet that is a poor criterion, because a sustainable use pattern can exist for reasons having little to do with management capabilities. If demand is low or if the capacity to exploit a resource is limited, the usage pattern may be perfectly sustainable, but this fortuitous outcome would be unrelated to institutional design. Institutions that coexist with sustainable patterns of usage in one situation may fail utterly in other situations. Although outcomes are obviously relevant, it is important to try to determine whether the governing institutions themselves enhance efficiency.

Efficiency is difficult to define. As Jules Coleman notes, there are three, possibly four, concepts used by economists to define efficiency (1988, 68). The definition that will be used here is *allocative efficiency,* which requires that resources be put to their most productive use.[14] An

---

13. Knight 1992 and Knight and Sened 1995 are among the exceptions.

14. There are other concepts of efficiency, some of which I will refer to later. An allocation of resources is said to be *Pareto optimal* if there is no other allocation that would make one individual better off without making another worse off. An allocation A is *Pareto superior* to an alternative allocation B if at least one individual is better off under A than under B and no one is worse off. A state of affairs is *Pareto suboptimal* if there is at least one alternative that is *Pareto superior* to it. Instead of *Pareto optimality,* economists often use *Kaldor-Hicks efficiency,* which states that a reallocation is efficient if and only if the surplus thus

efficiency-enhancing institution allows individuals to minimize transaction costs while reducing deadweight losses due to failures to cooperate in realizing potential gains from trade or cooperation. Among other things, they allow social actors to solve collective action problems. Whether an institution enhances efficiency is even more difficult to measure empirically. In examining the case of Washington fisheries, I must proceed circuitously by looking at the range of transaction costs the parties must meet, and comparing the institutions in use with the set of potential alternative institutions. A good example of the application of this method is Robert Ellickson's studies of the informal cost-sharing and liability rules used by Shasta County cattlemen and nineteenth-century whalers (Ellickson 1991, 1989). What this more flexible, commonsense approach loses in terms of empirical rigor, it more than gains by enlarging the range of phenomena that can be investigated.

I do not expect the institutions in use to be universally efficient, nor do I consider efficiency the only measure of successful collective action. In politics, unlike (perhaps) economics, there is no "filter of competition" that ensures that inefficient institutions are weeded out. Whatever pressures there are toward economic efficiency (and I believe there are some) are filtered, instead, through the pressures brought to bear by groups whose benefits are affected by the choice of institutions. To the extent that groups are heterogeneous and members expect different rules to have different distributional consequences, or where mechanisms for redistribution of the surplus are inadequate, this highly politicized process is likely to produce barriers to efficiency.

The creation and maintenance of institutions is also shaped by ideology: by what individuals consider to be fair or legitimate, what they believe about the world and what they believe the world should be. The principle of fairness, however defined, is to many people at least as compelling an ideal as efficiency. Institutions grounded in some version of equity might make allocative decisions based on financial need, historical claims, the absence of alternative sources of income or employment, or some other standard. Variations in culture affect the salience of different concepts of equity. Another principle stands apart from economic considerations or even those of equity. Decisions about who can fish, where and when, are intimately connected with issues of cultural identity for Indian fishermen.[15] Indians contend that fishing is a time-honored way of life, rather than simply a way of making a living. The fact that such claims may be made strategically as well as sincerely makes the researcher's task

---

generated would allow those who benefit to compensate those who lose. It is not necessary that they do so, only that they could do so. See Coleman 1988, chapters 3 and 4, for further discussion of the relationship between these different notions of efficiency.

15. Non-Indian fishermen make a similar claim, however.

more difficult, but it does not detract from whatever significance they might have.

It is not my intention to draw normative conclusions about the ultimate wisdom of favoring one principle over another or any particular combination of principles. By examining the formal and informal rules and practices in place and their evolution, what I hope to illuminate is how real individuals, subject to political pressures and limited by imperfect information, weigh these conflicting principles in choosing institutions.

CHAPTER 2

Early Institutions of the Pacific Northwest Tribes

Economic efficiency is a value that tends to be associated with modern societies, yet the early inhabitants of the Pacific Northwest had incentives to efficiently manage scarce resources that were at least as compelling as those facing individuals in advanced industrial societies. Spatiotemporal variability in the natural environment plus the difficulty of storing food for extended periods of time meant there were substantial potential gains to social cooperation and exchange, both within and between groups. Many of the institutions characterizing the societies of early inhabitants of the Pacific Northwest were directed toward facilitating such cooperation.

This chapter may be seen as an exercise in what Jules Coleman has termed "descriptive analytic law and economics," in which principles of economic efficiency are used as explanatory tools with which to understand existing rules (1988, 67)—in this case, institutions of Pacific Northwest native societies. I try to demonstrate that the institutions with which native people organized themselves reflect principles of allocative efficiency—that is, within the range of potential institutions, those that were chosen could be expected to contribute to the maximization of overall social wealth. In the concluding section, I try to draw some conclusions from this case concerning the social conditions under which socially efficient institutions might emerge and be maintained.

The account that follows has much in common with, as well as some points of departure from, Richard Posner's well-known analysis of law in primitive societies (1980). Like Posner, I argue that the structure of these institutions can be seen, in part, as responses to transaction costs. Unlike Posner, I do not find that statelessness resulted in the sort of high transaction costs that he attributes to it, nor do I find that transaction costs in general were especially high in such societies. Rather, I argue that various characteristics of such societies encouraged social cooperation and facilitated the emergence of institutions that performed the same transaction-cost minimizing role that Posner attributes to states, but without the myriad costs that accompany state creation and maintenance.

Posner argues, as I do, that insurance against risk was an important element of many native institutions. He states that various practices such as gift giving, reciprocal exchange, customary prices, and the size of kinship groups can be explained as "adaptations to uncertainty or high information costs" (Posner 1980, 4). He is primarily concerned with two kinds of information: (1) scientific knowledge or technology and (2) "information concerning the reputation, character or reliability of potential partners to exchange." He concludes that both sorts of information were costly in these societies relative to modern societies and that much of what is distinctive about institutions in aboriginal societies is attributable to this fact. While it seems entirely plausible to suggest that various native religious beliefs, or what some people would call superstitions, might arise in response to limited scientific knowledge, his second point is less convincing.

With respect to the costs of gathering information about potential partners, Posner's analysis seems to overemphasize the high costs of information in some areas while at the same time understating the characteristics in native societies that tended to lower information costs in others. Posner states that in primitive or stateless societies, it is costly to establish whether another party will fulfill a contract "since there are no courts to coerce his performance" and that that explains the existence of institutions such as kinship reciprocity, a norm of generosity and gift exchange between prospective trading partners (Posner 1980, 5). This argument is something of a sleight of hand, however, since it fails to take into account the *costs* of creating and maintaining a state, a court system, and all the accompanying institutions. In addition, creating a state entails strong asymmetries of power between the rulers and those they rule, and once in power, state actors may favor the interests of some groups over others (Bates 1981). My interpretation of the institutions of the native societies in the Pacific Northwest suggests that certain characteristics—low mobility, multistranded relations, shared beliefs, rough equality, in short, what was earlier described as *community*—allowed individuals to fashion institutions that facilitated whatever sorts of exchanges were feasible, given the constraints of limited transportation or communication, far more efficiently and equitably than a state would have done.

Transaction costs should be considered in the context of the transaction resources that groups are able to summon in meeting those costs (Heckathorn and Maser 1987). While the Posner argument is that the lack of centralized political authority resulted in high enforcement costs, which resulted in the development of institutions to compensate for this lack, my interpretation is that where communities were close-knit, and roughly egalitarian, enforcement costs were low and thus freed individuals from the necessity of creating a state.[1] That is not to say that transaction costs were insignificant; they were not, and some sorts of joint endeavors were obviously precluded by prohibitively high transaction costs, which the creation of a state might have alleviated.[2] But other sorts of costs were probably lower, as Posner himself seems to recognize at some points in his analysis, and the presence of a state would have likely undermined the social conditions that facilitated and maintained such institutions.

Contracts, property rights, and broader social institutions all arise from the efforts of individuals to construct a framework within which they can coordinate their joint activities, establish expectations concerning what others are likely to do, and protect themselves from strategic behavior stemming from asymmetric information and opportunism. For example, it is often both difficult and costly to determine with a high degree of accuracy the relative contributions of various inputs to joint production, and this difficulty is the basis of the shirking problem discussed in chapter 1, which is, of course, a type of collective action problem. An *efficient* contract is one that attempts to surmount this difficulty through the creation of incentives for those with greater information and control over the variability of a particular input to utilize that input most productively (Barzel 1989).

Realistically, it would be impossible to create incentive structures that *fully* maximize the contributions of all inputs in the context of a joint production or cooperative enterprises (Miller 1992). While joint production necessarily introduces some uncertainty about who is contributing what, without it, individuals would have to forgo the benefits of specialization. Another check on shirking or other sorts of opportunism is provided by social institutions that bind individuals into ongoing relationships and serve to make their long-term strategies interdependent. Social institutions, particularly if they are part of a larger network of institutions such as exists in a close-knit community, also facilitate the process of gathering information about the abilities and trustworthiness of others and ease the costs of monitoring and enforcement of agreements. Thus, contracts and

---

1. Obviously, there are other reasons for state formation, particularly threats from external forces.

2. Thrainn Eggertsson notes that technical change can help to lower transaction costs by introducing new methods of measurement, but that technical change is also associated with more complex commodities that result in higher transaction costs of exchange. He concludes that the small amount of systematic evidence that exists suggests that the net effect of technical change has been to increase the cost of transacting in advanced industrial countries (1990, 16).

broader social and political institutions each affect allocative efficiency, although they coexist in a state of creative tension. Efficiency in contracts involves designing incentive structures that closely align individual rewards with individual contributions. Broader social institutions can (ideally) create the conditions that allow people to solve collective action problems that lie beneath the surface of any joint production or collective effort, but they do so partly through linking an individual's welfare with the welfare of the larger group.

The following section describes the resource environment of the Pacific Northwest with respect to the challenges it created from the perspective of institutional design. Next, I discuss a number of key institutions—marriage customs, kinship networks, property rights, contracts, and the potlatch tradition—and evaluate their efficiency in light of these environmental parameters. Allocative efficiency would suggest that:

> Land use practices, contracts, division rules, and property rights should be structured in such a way so as to encourage investment in the resource, the accumulation of special skills, or the expenditure of effort when each could be expected to affect the productivity of the resource.
>
> Social institutions should reduce the costs of locating exchange partners, facilitate monitoring and enforcement of agreements and thus reduce transaction costs by lowering the costs of information. They should also mitigate opportunism by binding individuals into durable networks of interdependency, thus reducing the disjuncture between individual and collective rationality over the longer term.

The Political Economy of Coastal Salish Tribes

No student of the tribes of the Pacific Northwest has failed to note their high level of affluence during the precontact era. Population density was among the highest of any food-gathering people in North America (Suttles 1987, ch. 4), and art, architecture, and crafts were highly evolved. There is no question that aboriginal people of the Pacific Northwest were successful in adapting to their environment.

The basic unit of social organization was the *house group,* composed of one or more extended families who shared a large, cedar-plank longhouse during the winter months (Suttles 1987, ch. 2). A winter village might have as few as a dozen people or as many as a thousand. House groups within a village were only loosely affiliated, and during the summer months, individual families traveled to a series of temporary summer gathering sites. More important than village ties were extensive kinship networks (Suttles 1987, ch. 11; Onats 1984; Barsh 1991).

Like most so-called primitive societies, coastal Salish societies lacked formal or centralized political authority. While house groups generally had a leader, these individuals exercised little authority beyond the house or beyond particular spheres of activity. And while villages might under some circumstances unite against other groups and such conflicts generally followed territorial or linguistic boundaries, tribal identity was only infrequently salient; it was normally overshadowed by kinship.[3] No supragroup authority enforced agreements or maintained social order, yet there was considerable cooperation between individuals, households, and villages, even across tribal boundaries.

The material basis for these highly evolved and affluent societies was the availability of abundant food resources. These included shellfish, waterfowl, marine mammals such as whales, seals, and sea otters, land mammals such as elk, deer, bear, and beaver as well as berries, camas bulbs, and other plants (Suttles 1987, ch. 2). Most important of these resources were six species of salmon and steelhead. For most of the Coast Salish groups, these fish were the major staple food (Lane 1973). Some estimates put the average per capita consumption of salmon at 600 pounds per year (Hewes 1973, 136).

While such abundance was a necessary condition for a high level of material affluence, it was by no means sufficient (Suttles 1987, ch. 4). Indians of the Pacific Northwest Coast did not live in an earthly paradise free from material want, toil, planning, or the need to cooperate with others to achieve their goals. While food resources were concentrated, so was population. There are accounts of severe privation and near starvation, particularly among the upriver tribes and the tribes living along the outer coast (Collins 1950; see also the sources cited by Suttles 1987, 47–50). Salmon and other resources could be harvested in enormous quantities, but only during limited periods of time. Cyclical fluctuations are the rule for several species of salmon, and periodic shortages were not uncommon.

In short, the resource environment of the Pacific Northwest coastal region was capable of yielding great quantities of food, but it was highly variable. To prosper in this environment, native people needed to solve a number of organizational problems. In the section that follows, I will

---

3. Although the tribal names currently applied to the peoples under discussion were not used by them to describe themselves, in this study I will follow the normal practices among the anthropologists studying these societies and use modern tribal names as a convenient way of designating the loosely affiliated peoples of particular river drainages.

examine different sources of variability and how they structured native institutions.[4]

Environmental Sources of Variability

Spatial Variability

The area of the Pacific Northwest inhabited by the predecessors of today's tribes can be divided into three resource zones: (1) coastal, (2) saltwater bays and the mouths of the rivers draining into Puget Sound, and (3) mountainous areas. Even within the same zone, the availability of particular resources varied with topography, the proximity of salt water or freshwater, and local conditions of precipitation and temperature. Camas bulbs, berries, and fish, particularly shellfish, were not available everywhere, at least not in sufficient abundance. Bands living along the sheltered bays of Puget Sound and Hood Canal had year-round access to shellfish; coastal and inland tribes did not. Coastal bands hunted whales and other marine mammals and fished for halibut, while upriver tribes had access to mountain goats. Although nearly all groups relied heavily on salmon, the quantities in which it was available varied, and different species of salmon were present in different places or at different times.

Temporal Variability

Another source of variability was seasonal availability. A few resources were available throughout the year; most were not. Camas bulbs, sprouts, and berries could be gathered only during relatively short periods in spring or summer, and some migratory waterfowl were available only in spring and fall. The most important food resource for nearly all groups was salmon, which is an anadromous fish. Born in small freshwater streams or rivers, salmon migrate to salt water, where they spend most of their adult lives, and then return at maturity to their natal streams, where they spawn and die. As they return to spawning grounds, they can be harvested in vast quantities, but concentrations of particular runs may last only a relatively short period.

Periodic superabundance presented a paradox. Spatiotemporal unevenness meant that a temporary abundance often outstripped a resident population's ability to gather or process it. Especially in the case of

---

4. The following section on spatial and temporal variation draws on the work of Wayne Suttles, particularly "Coping with Abundance: Subsistence on the Northwest Coast," in his *Coast Salish Essays* 1987.

salmon spawning runs, where the resource is heavily concentrated and the available technology highly efficient, the harvest potential was often many times what a group might be able to use. To preserve fish for winter, it needed to be cut and dried, either over outdoor racks in the dry summer months or indoors during the rainy fall, when most tribes had the greatest access to salmon. The need to attract and organize labor—both to catch fish, which was done by men, and to preserve them, which was done by women—was probably a major concern (Romanoff 1985).

Spatial variations are relatively predictable, seasonal variations somewhat less so, and other types of variation were irregular or unpredictable. Pink salmon runs occur only on alternate years. Sockeye salmon, a species that was extremely important to several tribes, normally produce an extremely large run every four years, followed by much smaller runs in the following years. Periodic shortages or inclement weather were a source of entirely unpredictable variation. Acquiring insurance against risk, therefore, would have been a matter of some importance.

As the work of Wayne Suttles and other anthropologists makes clear, characteristics of the resource environment meant that it would have been difficult, if not impossible, for any single house group or village to provide for all of its needs entirely through utilization of its home territory (Richardson 1981; Onats 1984). There were potential gains from trade between house groups of different villages and from different resource zones. At the same time, there were significant barriers to trade because of the high costs of specifying and enforcing exchange agreements, and the lack of standardized measures for quality and quantity. Such costs could be lowered by trading with individuals with whom one expected to have an ongoing relationship, and in fact, most of the exchanges that did occur, occurred between members of kinship groups.

Another way to ensure access to a diverse resource base was through the development of social relationships that allowed individual families to migrate to various resource sites. Such relationships eliminated the need for costly measurement of trade goods or of monitoring the contributions of hired labor, although it sacrificed gains from specialization that an alternative strategy based on trade might offer. The strategy of individual families moving from site to site had another obvious advantage in that it reduced costs associated with shirking problems. Since each family produced for its own use, each family member had fewer incentives to free ride as well as better opportunities to monitor the efforts of other family members.

To sum up, the challenge posed to natives of the Puget Sound and Washington Coastal region was to gain access to a somewhat more diverse stock of resources than was available in their own fairly limited residence territories. That would allow for greater variety in food and other resources and would allow individuals to insure themselves against the risks posed by the uneven distribution of resources and fluctuations over time. There were several alternatives: trade of finished goods, contractual arrangements that would facilitate joint production, flexible property rights that would insure that individual families had access to widely dispersed raw resources, or some combination of the three. The most efficient institutions would be those that encouraged the optimal use of productive resources—human skills, effort, and the development and utilization of technology through the creation of appropriate incentive structures, but which were also finely tuned to the physical environment.

Social Institutions

Marriage

Whatever other benefits it may have bestowed on participants, among the bands of the Pacific Northwest, marriage constituted a long-term contract between families. Marriage established the basis for the ongoing exchange of food resources, finished goods, and labor, as well as enabling each family to claim usufructuary rights to the resource territories of the other (Suttles 1987; Barnett 1938). Through kinship ties, a family could gain access to the products of all three resource areas. Naturally, marriage to members of bands whose resource territories were particularly abundant or reliable or which offered complementary resources were especially sought after.

Oliver Williamson has noted that firms that enter into long-term contracts often "exchange hostages" as a way of demonstrating good faith and demonstrating credibility (Williamson 1983). Without such a mechanism, mutually advantageous relationships would be encumbered by the fact that each party would be able to foresee circumstances in which they could be vulnerable to opportunism on the part of the other. In the case of firms, "hostages" could include the development of special skill or technologies by one firm that would be difficult to utilize in any other relationship. The purpose of such a mechanism is to create a situation in which the prospects of each party are bound up with the fortunes of the other.

The Pacific Northwest tribes "exchanged hostages" through marriage. By relinquishing some proportion of the productive capacity of what was one of their most productive assets—healthy young adults—families were able to cement a long-term relationship of trade and reciprocal usufructuary rights to each other's resource sites. This relationship could even be extended beyond the life of the initial partners, since in the event of the death of one spouse, it was common for the surviving partner

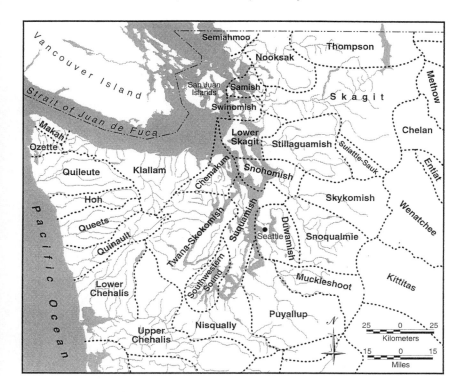

Map 1.   Locations of tribal territories at the time of contact. (*Map by Blake Feist.*)

to marry a sibling of the deceased spouse. Such a second marriage allowed the long-term contractual relationship to continue and minimized search and negotiation costs. The constellation of relationships among kinsmen on either side that had been established by the marriage could continue undisturbed.

Families tried to arrange marriages with others whose resident territories were some distance from their own. Village exogamy was the minimum; tribal exogamy was preferred. Individuals from poorer families had to be content with marrying other villagers. Wealthy families had extensive kinship networks extending to the islands, the tidal flats and river mouths, and the upriver areas including the mountains. Extensive kinship networks were thus both a cause and a consequence of wealth (Onats 1984).

Just as spatial variations were partially addressed through reciprocal usufructuary rights conveyed through marriage, so too was marriage useful in easing temporal fluctuations. One customary practice among the coastal Salish combined elements of trade and reciprocity. An individual with a temporary surplus of some food could bring it to the parents of his child's spouse, who were then bound to reward him and his helpers with "wealth" (durable, nonfood goods). This wealth was used at a later date to "thank" his relatives when they returned the favor with a similar gift of some food of which they had a temporary surplus. This exchange could also be practiced by other relatives, once it had been established through the initial gift exchange between co-parents-in-law. Marriage was thus of economic significance to a whole network of relatives.

Clearly such a practice helped groups insure themselves against risk. To fully appreciate the efficiency of this institution, however, consider the alternative uses to which a temporarily abundant resource could be put (see Suttles 1987, 18–20). A preservable commodity could be prepared and stored by the family or house group if sufficient labor was available. Doing so would eliminate the transaction costs associated with exchange—in this case, for example, there were likely to be uncertainties about whether the recipients were willing to "thank" the givers with an amount of wealth equivalent to the "gift." The outlays in time and effort necessary to preserve food were considerable, however, and it must have been the case that quite often all available laborers were already more productively occupied. Where a surplus was large, valuable, and occurred over an extended period of time, it is to be expected that some means of recruiting seasonal labor would evolve, but transaction costs would limit such developments to relatively few situations.

The other alternative use to which a surplus could be put was for the owner to hold a feast and invite other villagers. This action was used as a method of attracting new members to a house group, but of course that was not always a desired outcome.[5] By feasting other villagers or members of nearby villages, the host house could expect the favor to be returned at a later date, which made it a relatively low-cost way of building up "credit" for the future. Yet both the availability of surplus resources and the timing of such occasions of beneficence were apt to parallel the host's own circumstances. By moving beyond the immediate area for exchange partners, a family or house group could more effectively spread risk and widen the diversity of commodities available to it.

---

5. Wayne Suttles suggests that if a prosperous man was attracting more hangers-on than he wanted, he could, via his in-laws, convert the surplus into wealth, which he was not expected to redistribute. Thus, "a man's affines in other villages may have been his covert allies against potential spongers at home" (Suttles 1987, 60n.).

Property Rights among Northwest Coastal Indians

Northwest coastal Indians had a variety of property rights expressing different degrees of exclusivity, held by individuals, house groups, families linked through marriage, and members of villages. Individual, exclusive property rights existed in personal belongings and equipment and in knowledge of a spiritual, professional, or technological nature. Generally individuals owned their own labor power, although slavery did exist.[6]

A complex system of interlocking land and water rights linked individuals from different villages who were related through birth or marriage. Village members held primary rights over the areas within the territory surrounding their winter villages, which were normally located adjacent to productive salmon streams. People also had secondary rights to the resident territories of those to whom they were related by marriage and to the territories of the villages in which they were born.

In the fall and winter months, members of villages were often the exclusive users of their own fishing sites (Lane 1973). In spring and summer, they often fished and gathered cooperatively, and access rights of one sort or another were extended beyond the resident members of a community. In some cases, individuals who were outside this network of kinship could also ask to fish, hunt, or gather, and such permission was likely to be granted if it did not impinge on use by anyone else. This was not a situation of open access; cases where individuals attempted to use sites owned by others without receiving permission resulted in friction. Among the Kwakiutl, the northern neighbors of the Coast Salish who share many cultural attributes, trespass was reported to be sometimes punished by death (Lane 1973; Drucker 1957). There were also "in-common" areas that could be considered open access, however. They included deeper saltwater areas such as the Sound or the Strait of Juan de Fuca, which were used by many different tribes for passage routes and for winter salmon trolling.

Within a particular village territory, many hunting and gathering areas were freely available to any resident. Testimony of native people dating to the early contact period makes it abundantly clear, however, that the most productive fishing locations were owned by particular individuals or a group of closely related kinsmen (Stern 1934, 126, 127; Suttles 1987, Richardson 1981, 93). Ownership was heritable, generally from father to eldest son, and transferable, although in practice such transfers were

---

6. Among the Coast Salish, slaves (usually war captives) were relatively small in number. And since it is reported that slaves sometimes became too numerous, at which point they were freed and started new villages, it seems unlikely that slavery in general formed an important part of the economy. See Suttles 1987, esp. 3–14.

mainly confined to relatives, particularly sons-in-law during the exchange of gifts that constituted the wedding ceremony. Although it was possible to survive solely through access to common property, life was poorer and more insecure for those without access to the more productive, "owned" sites.

Property Rights and the Creation of Incentives

Among native people, property rights appear to have been specific to particular resource-gathering activities, which accounts for the difficulty that social scientists have had in trying to equate them with the more static property-rights regimes typical in modern, industrial societies. Property rights varied according to the type of resource present, the level of concentration of the resource, the type of equipment used, and how production was organized. In many respects, it is appropriate to think of property rights over resources and labor as a series of linked contracts that appear to have been designed to maximize overall productivity.

Where resources were spread relatively sparsely or there were no advantages to joint production, resource sites generally had open access to members of a resident group. For example, camas bulb areas were not normally owned by an individual or family. Although particular patches were dug each year by the women of one family or house group, there was no prohibition on use by others. The same was generally true of clam beds, yet in a few places where beds were particularly rich or where they were cultivated by clearing out stones and debris, they were said to be "owned" by one family. Clamming and digging for bulbs were activities that women frequently performed together, but they did not normally cooperate in the processing of these commodities. Generally, whatever the women of one family picked, they kept for themselves.

Tenure arrangements for hunting territories followed a similar pattern. When deer were hunted with a bow and arrow, men hunted individually or in pairs. While there was considerable skill involved in hunting, which was reflected in a certain amount of specialization of labor, there were no real advantages to large-scale cooperation using this method. An alternative method of hunting that involved the use of a large net did involve cooperative effort. In this case, the owner of the net organized and directed the hunt, although in neither case is there mention of hunting territories themselves being owned. Unfortunately, there are no records of how the proceeds of the hunt were allocated.

In his well-known study of the development of property rights among certain North American tribes, Harold Demsetz noted that under the conditions of increasing scarcity caused by increasing demand for furs by trappers, institutions of private property over hunting territories began to emerge (Demsetz 1967). No such development took place among the Pacific Northwest tribes, but there is no indication that hunting pressure had begun to press against the limits of carrying capacity. It is not surprising, then, that we find neither increased specification of individual or family property rights nor the presence of local rules limiting access such as have evolved in countless other examples of locally managed "commons" (McCay and Acheson 1987; Feeney et al. 1990). While there were elaborate rules, rituals, and taboos regarding the proper method of hunting (particularly for the larger, more ferocious animals), they were associated with enhancing individual prowess, not with ensuring collective restraint. Possibly the reason there was no "commons" problem nor institutions designed to prevent the emergence of one was that the time and effort involved in hunting land mammals in this terrain compared unfavorably with the effort-to-catch ratio of salmon fishing.

Neither clamming, berrying, camas bulb gathering, nor the most common method of hunting allows for greater output through the combination of different skills. Consequently there was no reason to encounter the transaction costs associated with disentangling the relative contributions of different workers. Nor could local users significantly affect the long-term productivity of the resource, given the technology at hand and given the fact that there appeared to be little threat of overreaching the carrying capacity. Thus, there was little to be gained by the establishment of either individual property rights or collectively enforced rules of use. Simply restricting use to residents and their kin was sufficient. The only aspect of production over which individuals could affect variability was the level of skill and effort in their own labor. Individuals did have property rights over that.

In general, then, where resources were thinly spread and thus relatively costly to defend,[7] where there were few economies of scale in either labor or equipment, or where long-term sources of variability were not subject to control by the individuals utilizing the resource, the property institutions were those of either open access or, more commonly, communal property open to members of the group, who were bound to extend usufructuary rights to kin. Short-term sources of variability in output were due either to natural forces (in which case, no particular set of institutional arrangements was any better than any other) or the amount of effort or skill employed by the individual hunter-gatherer. Since each individual or family kept whatever they produced, incentives to shirk were attenuated.

---

7. This finding is consistent with the economic defendability model introduced by anthropologists Rada Dyson-Hudson and Eric Alden Smith (1978).

Property institutions were quite different where resources were highly concentrated and where there were efficiency gains from large-scale cooperation in harvesting or preserving. For example, most bands received the bulk of their yearly supply of fish from weirs erected in the streams or rivers adjacent to their winter villages. Fishing weirs are barriers, usually made of logs or sticks, that prevent the upriver passage of salmon on their way to spawn. This is a highly efficient fishing method, but it requires the combined efforts of a number of workers. Construction of a weir might take members of a village or sometimes several villages as long as a month. Once completed, the weir created a barrier across a river or stream with a narrow walkway across the top. Fishing platforms large enough to accommodate a single fisherman extended from the basic structure.

The sites were always the private property of an individual (or perhaps a father and son or two brothers) who functioned as entrepreneurs, directing construction of the weir. The weir itself was considered the property of the village, and any village resident could fish from the top of it. Platforms were the property of individual families, as were the smokehouses built along the bank to facilitate the preserving of fish, particularly in the cool, damp autumn.

This sophisticated mixture of property rights is perfectly explicable once we consider what is demanded by efficiency in different activities or phases of the overall production process. The quality of construction of a fishing weir is a public good. The entire weir is affected by the strength of each section. Participants are affected by the degree of energy and skill other participants bring to bear on the task, yet each has incentives to shirk since the benefits of his own effort are nonexcludable and no one can control the effort others are devoting. Ceding authority to a single decision maker is one way of resolving this dilemma.

Once the weir has been constructed, there is no longer any efficiency advantage to joint production. In fact, the best way to ensure an optimal outlay of effort is to make individual workers the owners of what they produce. And in fact, stations or platforms along the weir were allocated to individual fishermen. There is little information on the criteria used to allocate these spots, but based on the underlying features of the Salish worldview,[8] it seems plausible that they were ceded to families who, over time, had shown themselves to be efficient fishermen.

---

8. In general, the Coast Salish believed that an individual's capacity to exploit a resource productively was attributable to his receiving "advice" from the spirits. Since being on good terms with the spirits was also what conveyed legitimacy on "ownership" claims, it would have seemed entirely right and proper for relatively well-off families to control fishing grounds, as long as they were generous. Obviously the Coast Salish are not the only society to believe that wealth was a sign of one's goodness in the eyes of deities. See Max Weber, *The Protestant Ethic* (1930).

Owners of sites were rewarded for their efforts through the creation of an obligation on the part of the other fishermen either to share the catch with the owner or reciprocate in some other way in the future. For example, rights to fish at the "owner's" site might require that an individual contribute wealth or provisions when the owner was planning to hold a potlatch. It also seems likely that ownership conveyed the right to fish from the most productive location, although the ethnographic record is inconclusive on this point.

Reef-netting Contracts

The design of labor contracts for reef-net fishing among various Straits tribes was a model for the optimal utilization of a highly efficient technology. The reef-net fishery was extremely important in the economy of the people of the Straits of Juan de Fuca and nearby areas (Suttles 1987), and modified aboriginal technology continued to be utilized well into the twentieth century.

The sockeye runs that pass through the Straits of Juan de Fuca in mid-July are large and highly concentrated. As they migrate through the waterways surrounding the hundreds of islands that make up what is now known as the San Juan Archipelago, they pass over various kelp-covered reefs lying close to the shorelines of various islands. Through a combination of finely honed skills and the employment of complex aboriginal technology, Indian fishermen were able to harvest up to 3,000 fish on a single cycle of the tide (Boxberger 1989).

Reef netting was practiced with a rectangular net, 30 to 40 feet long and 20 to 30 feet wide. Made from bark, its sections were constructed each year by the wives of the fishing crew members. It was dyed black so as to be camouflaged among the kelp beds. The reef net was suspended between two canoes in the water above the reef. Auxiliary lines running off from the ends of the net were anchored to large rocks that had been previously placed in strategic locations under the direction of the crew captain. Concealed with strips of kelp, these lines were used to create the optical illusion of a narrow passageway through the reefs, but they in fact guided the fish over the net. Once a sufficient number of fish were passing over, the net could be lifted, the two canoes drawn together, and the salmon unloaded into one of the canoes and transported to shore, where the women prepared the fish for drying on the large racks adjacent to the longhouse. The locations of these summer camps were chosen to take advantage of long hours of sunlight and prevailing winds. The amount of labor involved in weaving nets and cutting and drying fish probably equaled that spent building the trap and catching fish.

Reef-netting locations were always private, heritable property. The owner of a site was generally the crew captain, unless he was too old or infirm, in which case he remained at camp (to oversee the women drying salmon, perhaps) and appointed someone else to assume the responsibilities of captain. When out on the reef, it was the owner-captain's job to stand in the offshore canoe and watch for fish. When the captain saw the fish approaching, he thanked them for their appearance and urged them closer. Once they were in proper position, he directed the efforts of the crew in hauling in the lines and lifting the net. On the water or off, the captain wore a special hat, which he hung on a pole as he entered the house to signify that he was watching the salmon even when he was not fishing (Stern 1934, 43). The skill and knowledge of the captain were important elements of successful fishing. For example, to properly situate the anchor rocks, the captain needed to be very familiar with the geography of the ocean floor and the prevailing currents. Knowing exactly when to pull up the nets was also critical.

Ethnographic accounts of the contractual arrangements associated with the reef-net fishery are quite clear. Each owner hired a crew, who tended to be drawn from the pool of available relatives, although an owner "might hire anyone who came asking to work for him" (Stern 1934, 46). Each crew member was required to furnish a section of net, which was constructed by his wife. Wives also prepared and dried the fish. The owner furnished the two canoes and hired hunters to supply the camp with meat. (Presumably the meat was needed during the period of time before the runs began, when nets were being constructed and various other preparatory tasks completed.) Each crew member received a share of the catch. As recounted by Stern (1934, 46), a particular way of allocating the fish was observed:

Ten piles of fish are made for the 10 men participating and as the catch is distributed, the captain must count, 'one-one, two-two, three-three,' and so on repeating each number up to 10 as he deposits ten fish in each pile before he goes onto the next one. After he has dropped 10 fish in each of the piles, he begins with the first one until the entire catch is allotted. The fish are distributed after each haul, until each person participating obtains his share. Then the rest of the fish, comprising the largest portion, belong to the owner of the site. No matter how early in the season a person obtains his share, he must continue in the party until the season, which extends through July and August, is over. There is much work to be done after the fishing is completed and each person participating must help in this work.

Clearly this is a fairly sophisticated arrangement, which combines aspects of share and wage contracts and allows all parties to take advantage of specialization between hunters, fishermen, and owners of capital. Both reef owners and crew members controlled different assets affecting the variability of the output. Owners could be expected to have greater knowledge about the particular characteristics of the site, such as the condition of the ocean floor, currents, and the like. Thus, an owner was the logical party to interpret the currents and tides and direct the crew's efforts in preparing the site and in catching the fish. As the "residual claimant," he had incentives to expend considerable effort in ensuring a productive season. And since owners were generally wealthy men, they were better equipped to bear the initial costs of furnishing supplies for the group. The incentives for each team of crew member and his wife to use the skills and energy they had available are apparent in the first phase of the contract. In the crew member's case, he had a substantial stake in the overall catch. In the case of the female partner, the amount preserved and stored for family consumption was directly proportional to her own skill and effort.

A puzzle remains. Given that crew members' portions were distributed early in the season, what kept crew members and their wives from packing up and moving on to some other resource site after they had secured their share? Such a threat would seem to have appeared credible and would have allowed crew members to use their position to hold up owners for a larger share at any point in the season. At the very least, this contractual arrangement would seem to encourage shirking during the latter stages when crew members were working solely for the owner. Why was the contract set up in such a way as to leave reef owners vulnerable to any of these outcomes, especially when there was an obvious alternative available in the form of a fixed owner–crew member share contract in effect throughout the season?

There are several, not necessarily competing, explanations. One is that being a member of a reef-net crew was sufficiently desirable that individuals were unwilling to jeopardize future crew opportunities by defecting in one season; the presence of multifaceted relations, shared values, low discount rates, and the expectation of continued interaction with the same set of members was sufficient to make defection unlikely in this as in other situations where parties enter into agreements or jointly provide collective goods. While some level of community is probably a necessary condition for the endogenous resolution of various collective action problems present in contracting, it does not explain why this and not some other, less-testing form of contract was chosen.

Is there a positive contribution such a contract could have made?

That seems possible once the contract is examined from the perspective of the crew members. Sockeye salmon have a quadrennial cycle; a very large run in one year is followed by a much smaller run in the subsequent year and two very-small-run years after that. The difference between the smallest and largest years may be a factor of several thousand (Boxberger 1989). It is possible that in the two years of smallest runs, the total catches barely covered the crew shares; and in the one-in-four extremely large-run years, the owner did very well. (Unfortunately, the ethnographic record is not sufficiently detailed on this point; we have no way of knowing whether the described allocation, in which "the largest share was left over for the owner," was a low- or high-yield year. Given the transaction costs of switching from one form of contract to another or even of predicting the run size, it is likely that the same sharing arrangement prevailed from year to year.) In any case, it seems quite plausible that crew members insisted on a share contract that would protect them in the worst years, and for this protection they were willing to relinquish claims on surpluses created in plentiful years.[9] The owner was able to convert the surpluses created in plentiful years into wealth, which could subsequently be used to hire hunters and otherwise underwrite the expenses of the group.

The peculiar shape of this contract has another positive attribute. Measuring the potential output of a worker and trying to detect shirking is a difficult problem. Direct supervision of the crew by the owner partially solves this problem, but supervision is costly and never complete (Barzel 1989). A more accurate measure of optimal output is provided by letting workers keep more of what they produce. In addition, there was the other, equally important and time-consuming aspect of production—the cutting and drying of fish—which most experts have estimated took as long as fishing. If the owner was directing the harvesting effort, he could not at the same time directly supervise the women preserving the fish, although presumably the women of his household could. An additional check on the level of potential productivity or optimal effort for both crew members and their wives could be provided by using the initial level of productivity—when they each were working solely for their own households—to set the standard for the subsequent period.[10] Thus a contract such as was in

---

9. It seems likely that native people would have attributed cyclical variations to supernatural forces. Since the captain (who wore the salmon-watching hat) was the main intermediary with the gods, it was consistent with native ideology that he would receive a very large share during a particularly good year.

10. See Barzel 1989 from which this analysis draws, for an explanation of how monitoring costs affected the implicit labor contract between slaveholders and slaves in the American South.

place for reef netting would have tended to minimize the problem of measuring output and reducing shirking.

The Exceptional Makah

Environmental conditions were somewhat different for one important tribe in the area. If the thesis that I have presented—that aboriginal institutions appear to enhance efficiency—is correct, then these variations should result in differences in their important institutions. The Makah, who are the southernmost member of the Nootkan peoples,[11] are located on the Northwestern tip of what is now the contiguous United States and are the only local tribe for whom salmon was not the major source of food (Singh 1966, 7; Lane 1973). Instead, the Makah caught and preserved halibut from banks located 5 to 30 miles offshore and hunted whales, sea lions, and other marine mammals. They lived in large, permanent villages and depended heavily on trade.

For tribes whose home territories were in the bays or along the rivers that drained into Puget Sound, the problem of spatiotemporal fluctuations could be solved through the establishment of kinship relationships that were, in effect, exchanges of long-term usufructuary rights to areas with various resources. Establishing such relationships also allowed for efficient utilization in situations of periodic superabundance because it facilitated the mobility of labor. Because of numerous navigable rivers around Puget Sound, the costs of transporting whole households across resource zones—as opposed to simply transporting products as would be the case with trade—were not terribly great.

The Makah faced a somewhat different resource environment. The interior of the northwestern Olympic Peninsula receives more than 100 inches of rainfall yearly and the vegetation is characterized by dense, nearly impenetrable forests with few easily navigable rivers. The cycle of yearly food-harvesting activities was not dominated by predictable periods of superabundance, as was the case with the Puget Sound tribes with respect to salmon runs. And unlike weir fishing, where stations along the weir can be used by a number of fishermen (in some cases, fishermen fished in shifts in order to more productively utilize the weir) without additional cost, each whaling crew or group of halibut fishermen must be separately

---

11. The Makah spoke a language that was part of the Wakashan family, quite distinct from the Salishian language group of the other tribes under discussion here. In terms of culture and patterns of social organization, the Makah are classified as a Nootkan tribe, who had close associations with the other Nootkan tribes of Vancouver Island. See Drucker 1951 for more on the Makah.

equipped. Thus, the challenge of periodic superabundance and the consequent for mobility did not loom nearly as large in the Makah economy. It is not difficult to understand why Makah house groups tended to migrate only from winter to summer villages, rather than following the more common pattern of seasonal migration along routes established and maintained by kinship affiliation.

It was suggested earlier that trade offers an alternative economic strategy to the kinship-based system of migration and reciprocal usufructuary rights. Given the environmental constraints facing the Makah, it is not surprising that commerce was extremely important in their economy.[12] The Makah were a medium for trade between the other Nootkan tribes of the north, the tribes along the coast, and the inland Columbia River tribes. They traded goods of their own—whale oil, blubber, and dried halibut— and goods that had been previously acquired through trade from the Nootka to the north and the Chinook, a tribe located up the Columbia River. The volume of such trade in precontact days can only be estimated, but the government figures for 1852 cite a figure of 20,000 gallons of fish and whale oil sold by Makahs to whites. Swan estimates a much lower figure of 5,000, but all accounts agree that the Makah were highly active traders, both before and after contact with whites (Swan 1870, 30).

There are significant transaction costs associated with trade, particularly with respect to enforcement. One way to meet these costs is to invest in a reputation for prompt and severe retaliation. The Makah were described by early Europeans as a "fierce and difficult" people. And at a time when sheer force of numbers was the most important determinant of military might, the Makah were a large tribe whose members were spatially concentrated in five large villages.

Property Rights among Nootkan Tribes

Much has been written about the extensive domain over which the Makah and other Nootkan tribes had property rights. As Philip Drucker (1951, 247) states,

> The Nootkans carried the concept of ownership to an incredible extreme. Not only rivers and fishing places close at hand, but the waters of the sea for miles offshore, the land, houses, carvings on a house post, the right to marry in a certain way or the right to omit

---

12. The Makah relied heavily on trade with the Nootkan tribes of Vancouver Island, even to the extent of obtaining from them the large, expertly designed canoes they used for whaling.

part of an ordinary marriage ceremony, names, songs, dances, medicines, and rituals, all were privately owned property.

The Makah valued marine property more than property in land, which is not surprising given the relative productivity of the two sorts of resource territories in the area. Property rights in inshore waters were identified by reference to mountaintops and other natural landmarks. The head of a house group owned the house, the adjacent beach, and salvage rights to whatever washed up on that beach, including whales. As anthropologist Barbara Lane (1973, 26) notes,

> Worse yet, they equally seized and claimed as their booty any survivors of these shipwrecks. This behavior was evidence to whites of the cupidity and savagery of the Makah. Actually, it was the exercise of well-defined property rights among the Nootkan peoples . . .

Chiefs were the nominal owners of whatever property was owned, although it would be more accurate to say that as heads of particular kinship groups, chiefs managed group-owned resources (Richardson 1981, 103). Rights to a certain cut of blubber from a whale washed up along a particular stretch of shore or the right to the second harvesting of berries at a particular patch are mentioned by Drucker as rights that a chief might give to a lesser chief, who in turn was required to present the owner with a portion of the output. Members of a chief's group were allowed free access to a particular resource after the chief had formally declared a seasonal opening. Either the first harvest or two or, in the case of halibut or salmon, a portion of the dried product was collected by the chief, who used it to give a large feast during which his claim to the property was affirmed. In practice, then, the owner of the resources in a particular territory functioned as a sort of entrepreneur or manager, an arrangement quite similar to that among the Puget Sound tribes.[13]

Division Rules

Many property rights were inherited, but many of the rules used by the Makah had the objective of rewarding industry and skill. For example, most animals that were hunted were the property of the hunter, to be disposed of by him in accordance with division rules based on relative contri-

---

13. The impression that "owners" functioned as corporate managers is strengthened by accounts of a potlatch custom in which a chief would report to those assembled what portion of the wealth he was distributing came from particular properties (Drucker 1951).

butions. The division of a harpooned whale was similar. Typically, the choice portion called the saddle went to the captain of the whaling canoe that had killed the whale. Other parts went to other hunters in a prescribed order determined by the order in which they had come to help him (Waterman 1920). Singh reports that the division of a whale among members of a successful canoe "reflected who had done the most work" (Singh 1966, 57). Sea otter hunting was done by surrounding an otter by perhaps 20 canoes and then shooting it with arrows. The hunter who killed the otter took possession of it, but he gave 10 pairs of blankets to the person whose arrow struck it second, 5 pairs to each of the others, and 5 to the one who harpooned it (Drucker 1951, 47–48, cited in Suttles 1987, 242). Similar rules govern some, although not all, cooperative hunting.

An efficient contract or division rule is one that encourages those who have the greatest potential to affect the output to do so. Where outcomes are largely dependent on random events—such as whales washing up on shore—any division rule will serve to increase efficiency by reducing confusion and potential conflict between competing claimants, thus claims to stranded whales were based on territorial rights. But where output can be affected by the parties, the incentive structure needs to encourage skill and effort. Skill and effort were rewarded by giving hunters property rights over the animals they killed. Hunting whales or other marine mammals is highly dangerous, and once one party seems assured of taking a whale, other hunters will be tempted to hang back instead of assisting them with the result that the prey (and perhaps the canoe and its crew) may be lost. Providing incentives to helpers minimizes these sorts of deadweight losses. The fact that the Makah distinguished between these two sorts of situations—beached whales and hunted whales—highlights the efficiency of their institutions.[14]

The Potlatch

Few Pacific Northwest native practices have attracted as much attention and generated as many explanations as the potlatch, the custom in which one or more house groups invited other bands to several days of feasting and dancing, culminating in the host group giving wealth to the visitors, generally in some prescribed order that reflected the visitors' status and relationship to the giver. At some later date, the guests reciprocate, but the potlatch was not designed to bank wealth for the future, as were "gifts" of

---

14. Robert Ellickson (1989) finds a similar pattern in the norms governing nineteenth-century whaling in New England.

food between in-laws. Unlike affinal exchange, the potlatch was fiercely competitive, and considerable wealth was given away or, in some cases, destroyed in an attempt to outdo the prior "generosity" of others. At first glance, this custom seems quite inconsistent with the principle of efficiency or social wealth maximization.

One group of anthropologists explains the existence of the potlatch as a functional response to the need for insurance against risk in an uncertain and variable natural environment (Piddocke 1965; Suttles 1987). Tribes whose hunting and gathering seasons had been very productive held potlatches that redistributed goods to tribes who had poorer seasons. A wealthy tribe gained status; a poorer tribe received the materials it needed to survive. Yet the occurrence of potlatches does not seem to be correlated to patterns of hardship among other tribes. If the potlatch functioned as a type of social insurance, it would be reasonable to expect that shortages in one village would elicit potlatch invitations from another and that potlatching would decrease as tribes became wealthier after contact and trade with Europeans and consequently had less need for insurance against risk. Neither of these things happened.

Helen Codere explains the potlatch as a surrogate for warfare; a type of ceremonialized "fighting with property" (Codere 1967), although some authors have argued that her account omits many cases of actual warfare and fails to note the economic interests that motivated such conflicts. Another explanation is that potlatching and warfare were both motivated at least in part by desires for economic gain. Specifically, they were closely related strategies to control productive resource territories (Ferguson 1983, 1984; Johnsen 1986). Most accounts of the potlatch agree that a large part of their purpose was to provide a forum in which to assert or reassert a claim, often a hereditary claim to a name or title, which in turn conveyed certain rights such as ownership of a valuable salmon stream (Drucker 1951; Suttles 1987; Barnett 1967). As Suttles (1987, 21) writes,

> By potlatching a group established its status vis-a-vis other groups, in effect saying, "we are an extended family (or a village of several extended families) with title to such-and-such a territory having such-and-such resources."

Guests were called upon to witness such events and were given wealth in exchange for their participation. By accepting the wealth, they, in effect, accepted the claims. In a situation where there were competing claimants for a resource territory, the claimant who could best his rival by giving away more wealth would be accepted as the rightful owner. According to Drucker (1967, 105–6),

The one who had been surpassed had no recourse. He could no longer contest his claim, for, in the native mind, it came to be regarded as ridiculous that an individual of few resources should attempt to make a claim against someone who had demonstrated power and wealth.

Potlatches can be conceived of as a mechanism by which winners could compensate losers for relinquishing their claims on income-generating property. Potlatching thus represents a more efficient means of securing property rights than warfare, not only because it eliminates unnecessary bloodshed, but also and more importantly because it sets up a superior criterion—a demonstrated capacity to amass wealth, as opposed an advantage in military prowess—for the right to control and organize the exploitation of resources.[15]

Efficiency and Redistributive Institutions

In this chapter I have attempted to demonstrate that the institutions of native people of the Pacific Northwest were generally efficiency-enhancing. I make no claim that this account is either conclusive or complete, that it either proves that these institutions were the most efficient ones available or that it illuminates the processes by which they evolved in the direction of maximizing social wealth. It would obviously be preferable if I could present evidence about an even wider range of economic activities or about the process of institutional change. But the ethnographic record is simply too sketchy to provide a series of "snapshots" of these institutions over time, and much of what does exist is simply not relevant to the kinds of questions being asked here.

The picture that emerges from glimpses of what were unquestionably the most important institutions of the Puget Sound and Pacific Northwest Coastal tribes supports the argument that they facilitated social wealth maximization. The structure of incentives created by native property rights, division rules, and labor contracts encouraged allocative efficiency by creating incentives for each participant to extend his or her best efforts. Where output could be affected by the development of skills and knowledge, economic and legal institutions were shaped to reward the accumulation of such skills or knowledge, and where the productivity of a

---

15. There are other explanations of the potlatch. D. Bruce Johnsen (1986) argues that the potlatch functioned as a way to establish property rights that were necessary to prevent the overexploitation of salmon runs. Since I am not convinced that (1) native fishing was a significant threat to the resource or (2) native resource managers were fully aware of the connection between overfishing in one year and shortages in some subsequent year, I find this explanation unconvincing.

resource could be affected by human effort and investment, the definition of property rights tended to reflect that. Social institutions reduced the costs of locating exchange partners, facilitated migration across resource territories, and lowered the costs of enforcement. Moreover, social institutions such as marriage made families interdependent, which helped resolve potential free-rider problems. In short, the Pacific Northwest tribes were very effective in solving various collective action problems. Why was that so?

Solving collective action problems entails meeting certain transaction costs—the costs of gathering information and specifying, monitoring, and enforcing an agreement. Native people were able to meet these costs because their relations with one another were characterized by community—common belief systems, multifaceted relations, and the shared expectation that they would continue to interact with one another over extended periods of time (Taylor 1982). Their membership in communities gave them certain social resources, by virtue of which many of the transaction costs that stand in the way of socially efficient institutions were reduced. Furthermore, the institutions themselves helped reinforce the very characteristics that allowed them to function efficiently.

Several key features of aboriginal social structure contributed to the emergence of efficient institutions. Individuals within groups were in fairly symmetric positions with respect to one another. While there were differences in wealth between individuals, they were not vast, and there were a number of leveling institutions that kept wealth inequalities more or less in check. At the same time, there were opportunities for upward mobility, through either marriage into a good family or hard work or talent. This combination of leveling institutions plus opportunities for exceptionally talented or hardworking individuals, added to the fact that individuals benefited from the prosperity of relatives scattered throughout an area, meant that the usual bargaining problems encountered when potential cooperators seek to choose among cost and benefit-sharing agreements were attenuated. Blocking an agreement or withholding consent from a practice that would maximize social efficiency was not likely to be a rational strategy in a situation where an individual or some member of his or her immediate family could have a reasonable expectation that he or she might directly benefit from any of a broad range of cost-benefit sharing arrangements or division rules, either in the present or in the future. Also, he or she could expect to benefit indirectly from the prosperity of other members of his or her kinship network, which was often quite large.

The complex system of property rights, contracts, and division rules that existed among the aboriginal people of the Pacific Northwest was finely tuned to the requirements of efficiency. If the state of scientific knowledge and the available technology with respect to transportation, communication, and production is taken as given, production and exchange associated with the utilization of this important resource were probably organized more efficiently than they are today. Individual incentive structures that were created under aboriginal social institutions appear to be more consistent with the maximization of aggregate wealth than are their equivalents in modern fisheries. This efficiency was made possible by the fact that particular rules were part of a complex of institutions that ensured that, in general, an individual could not significantly improve his or her own position without improving the fortunes of many others. While such a society may not have provided the sort of environment that encouraged technological breakthoughs that might have been forthcoming with a different set of social structures,[16] they did succeed in minimizing transaction costs and opportunistic behavior.

---

16. Some definitions of what would constitute efficiency-enhancing institutions would entail the creation of incentives to encourage innovation and entrepreneurial risk taking. Along with those, however, come an increase in at least some sorts of transaction costs and a decrease in some sorts of transaction resources.

CHAPTER 3

Development of the Salmon Fishery:
Mid-Nineteenth Century to the Present

The political, economic, and social institutions that allowed Pacific Northwest coastal tribes to flourish were no match for the onslaught of European civilization. Diseases such as smallpox and influenza drastically reduced aboriginal populations, the influx of large numbers of white settlers forced tribal people off their land, and the availability of new markets, products, and technologies eroded preexisting relationships of exchange and cooperation. New structures of power either replaced or were superimposed on traditional lines of political authority, altering them in unforeseen ways. Over the next century, Indians were pushed to the margins of the fishery, and government transfer payments or wage labor replaced fishing and gathering as the dominant features of tribal economic life. The fishery itself came under increasing pressure, first from overfishing and eventually from the deterioration of fish habitat due to hydroelectric power development, logging, and demands on rivers and tributaries for water for agricultural uses. Several trends in state fisheries management became apparent: a reluctance to preserve fish habitat if doing so involved crossing swords with well-organized interests, a heavy reliance on fish hatcheries to staunch losses due to declining natural runs, and a strong preference for forcing the heaviest burden for conservation onto a group of users who were politically powerless—the Indians.

Early Development of Salmon Fisheries

The Stevens Treaties, 1854–55

In a period of barely seven months beginning in December 1854, Isaac Stevens, governor of the Washington Territories, negotiated five treaties with representatives of the various indigenous peoples of the Pacific Northwest. The prospect of conducting separate negotiations with hundreds of small, politically autonomous bands must have appeared too time-consuming for political leaders seeking to facilitate territorial expansion, and so the treaty-making process was expedited by lumping various groups into "tribes" and appointing "chiefs" authorized to speak for them. Some tribal representatives refused to sign the treaties that had been drawn up for them, decisions that were to prove costly when the treaties were belatedly enforced some 120 years later.

Key components of all treaties negotiated with Pacific Northwest tribes were nearly identical. In exchange for ceding all their territory except what was held back for reservations, the Indians received lump-sum payments and yearly annuities. They were to be provided with teachers and schools, agricultural implements, sawmills, carpenters' and black-smiths' shops, and doctors. Most importantly from their perspective, they were to be allowed to continue their customary way of making a living through fishing and gathering. Both the interpreters and Governor Stevens himself were well aware of how dependent the tribes were on fishing, and they assured the signers that their customary subsistence patterns could continue to be followed both on and off the reservations. At the Point No Point Treaty signing, Governor Stevens is reported to have waved the treaty document in the air and proclaimed to the assembled Indians, "This paper secures your fish" (Cohen 1986, 37). Since the treaty language was English, and the negotiations conducted in Chinook, a "language" of some 300 words used for trading, these demonstrations were particularly important in shaping the perceptions of tribal people about what the treaties were intended to convey.

Such promises no doubt appeared harmless enough at the time. Neither the territories nor the fisheries were crowded, and Indians, with highly efficient technology and great expertise, were the primary suppliers of fish to settlers and traders, an arrangement that was mutually advantageous. Once the opportunities for large-scale commercial fishing and fish processing became apparent in the latter half of the nineteenth century, traditional Indian fisheries were gradually displaced by white fishermen using more expensive deepwater gear. For more than a century, the Stevens treaties were interpreted as conveying nothing more to natives than the same open-access rights enjoyed by white inhabitants. Since most Indians were unable to secure credit, they were unable to obtain the larger boats and more expensive gear that would have allowed them to compete in the deepwater, open-access fishery. By the period of 1936–56, the Indian catch was on average only about 1 percent of the state's commercial salmon catch (Washington State Department of Fisheries 1957, 61).

Economic Development of the Fishery

The first U.S. cannery was built in Puget Sound in 1877, and by the end of the century, Puget Sound was the center of cannery operations in the

Pacific Northwest (Netboy 1974, 350). Initially, the resource appeared so abundant that only chinook and sockeye salmon were used for canning—other species were simply dumped into the bays. Even when fishermen targeted exclusively on choice species such as sockeye, difficulties in making predictions about the size of runs and coordinating effort and demand meant that a great deal of excess fishing took place. Reporting on the sockeye catch of 1901, the commissioner of fisheries for British Columbia noted that canneries on both sides of the international boundary not only filled every can they could obtain, but it was believed that more salmon were thrown away than used (cited in Roos 1991, 13). Output during the early years was prodigious. In 1913, the last year before a rock slide nearly decimated the Fraser River runs, 2,752,866 cases of salmon were packed in Puget Sound in addition to those that were sold fresh, smoked, or frozen (Washington State Department of Fisheries 1924, 5). Nearly 40 million fish were caught in that year within Puget Sound alone (Washington State Department of Fisheries 1924, 24).

By this time, most of the Puget Sound canneries were being supplied with fish by white fishermen using traps modeled on traditional Indian weirs. Western technology made it possible to construct deepwater traps, and consequently trap operators were able to intercept fish headed upriver to traditional Indian fisheries. Fish traps were expensive to construct but highly efficient. A single trap harvested 50,000 fish, and some Puget Sound traps caught as many as 40 tons in a season (Barsh 1977, 23). Not surprisingly, the average price for a site was high, and by 1917, some sites were selling for over $100,000. A site owner could expect to recoup his investment in two or three years of fishing (Barsh 1977, 24).

Salmon can be harvested using a variety of methods, however, and fish-trap operators were vulnerable to the same strategy of interception they themselves had practiced against native fishermen. Both gillnetters and purse seine boat operators intercepted fish that otherwise would have been caught by trap operators. When traps are operated alone, they are highly efficient, but since they operate *behind* other gear types, their efficiency declines substantially with competition (and interception) from these other gear types. In fact, while purse seiners were less than half as efficient (as measured by the ratio of inputs to outputs) as traps operating alone, they were nearly twice as efficient as traps when the two gears operated together (see Barsh 1977, 31 for the figures on efficiency; the relative efficiency comparisons were computed by the author). And by 1920, large numbers of fish were being intercepted by ocean trollers before they could reach the net fishery (Barsh 1977, 26). Trolling is the least efficient and most indiscriminate method of fishing since it operates in mixed-stock areas (areas where fish from different stocks or breeding populations inter-

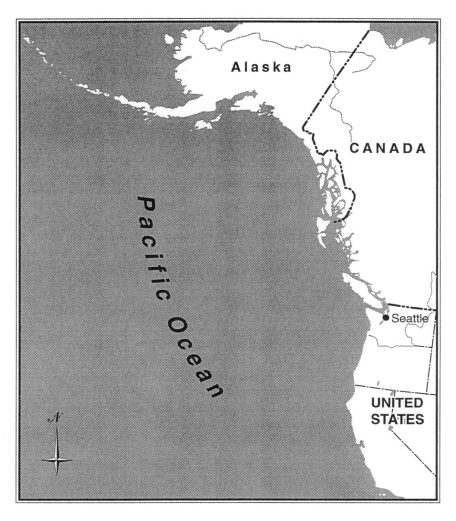

Map 2.   Range of Pacific salmon. (*Map by Blake Feist.*)

mingle) and takes considerable numbers of immature fish. By consistently failing to control entry, state regulatory agencies had allowed a pattern of earlier and earlier interception to develop, which ensured that more-efficient fishing methods would be systematically displaced by those that were less efficient (Higgs 1982).

Regulation of the Fishery

Fishing was regulated by season beginning in 1877, and time and gear restrictions became increasingly common in the late nineteenth and early twentieth centuries. There is evidence that such restrictions were customarily ignored by fishermen, however, and the state legislature was unwilling to commit resources either toward enforcement of ordinances or toward developing the scientific expertise necessary to manage salmon more effectively. Knowledge of even the basic rudiments of salmon life cycles and habitat requirements was lacking at this time. According to Crutchfield and Pontecorvo's classic study of the Pacific salmon fisheries,

> [A]s best as we can determine from the dim record, most of the regulations promulgated in the state of Washington were based on an intuitive feeling that certain types of gear were excessively destructive, or were undertaken in response to the interests of one pressure group or another. (Crutchfield and Pontecorvo 1969, 130)

Since Indian fisheries were highly visible and Indian fishermen politically powerless, they generally bore the brunt of these ill-informed regulatory schemes. The state legislature responded to public perceptions of overfishing by severely restricting fishing in rivers and tributaries—traditional tribal fishing areas.[1] In addition, the state restricted spearing and snaring, which were low-cost methods of fishing used primarily by Indians (Cohen 1986, 42).

By 1921 it was clear that the fishery was already seriously overcapitalized, yet the newly created Department of Fisheries was reluctant to limit entry. Instead, like fisheries management agencies the world over when faced with a problem requiring difficult political choices, it sought a less painful solution. Despite the state of near ignorance concerning salmon biology, Department of Fisheries officials evinced steadfast faith in the potential for fish hatcheries to mitigate damage to salmon caused by overfishing or habitat destruction. In 1913, a state representative initiated

---

1. In 1889, the Washington State Legislature closed six rivers to commercial salmon fishing, and over the next 20 years, all Puget Sound tributaries were closed to all but sport fishermen (Morishima 1987).

what was to become a common practice in resolving the conflict between hydroelectric power development and the requirements of salmon. Washington State Fish Commissioner Darwin suggested to the Olympic Power Company that it contribute to a fish hatchery in lieu of fulfilling its obligation under state law to construct fish passage facilities that would allow fish to reach upriver spawning streams above its dam along the Elwha River.[2] Eventually, more than 50 major dams would be constructed throughout the region. Some, such as the huge Grand Coulee Dam along the Columbia River, shut off 1,100 miles of spawning streams (Wilkinson 1987, chap. 5). To the extent that adverse affects on salmon were considered at all, it was assumed that hatcheries could mitigate the damage.

Competition between fishermen of different gear types was heated from the onset, and its protagonists managed to mine into several unrelated, but similarly conflictual social divisions.[3] The conflict over access to the fishery was marked by accusations and counteraccusations of overexploitation. As the most visible source of depletion, trap owners attracted the most public criticism for overfishing. With probably greater justification, they leveled the same charge against the purse seiners, who were the dominant user group in the seasons of 1914 and 1915 and took a greater proportion of immature fish. At the same time, the large and powerful group of sport fishermen were becoming increasingly vehement in their denunciation of trap owners. Once sport fishermen joined purse seiners and cannery operators (who by this time had seen the handwriting on the wall), their combined political strength plus public distrust for symbols of wealth and privilege were enough to turn the tide against the trap operators. In 1934, state voters passed an initiative banning fish traps and restricting commercial fishing to gill nets in southern Puget Sound. Although initially this initiative resulted in higher escapement levels, that effect continued only as long as it took for other user groups to expand. One study concludes that the major effect of Initiative 77 was to facilitate

2. Shortly thereafter, the state law was changed so that it expressly allowed hatcheries to be built in lieu of fish ladders. In the next few years, seven hatcheries were accepted in place of fish passage facilities on several area rivers. Most of these hatcheries, including the one on the Elwha, were later abandoned as failures. For the details on this and other developments in the early history of salmon in the region, see Brown 1982, especially chapters 4, 5, and 6.

3. Fish traps were capital-intensive and highly efficient. They tended to concentrate wealth in a few individual or corporate hands and were generally controlled by members of the local social and economic elite. Purse seining and gillnetting required little capital and thus provided economic opportunities for recently arrived Scandinavian immigrants. Economic competition between fishermen using different gear types was played out with a strong overlay of class and ethnic politics. In addition, trap owners, both because of the scale of their operations and their close affiliation with canneries, were seen as an obstacle to the other fishermen's collective struggle to get higher prices for fish.

a redistribution of the catch in direct proportion to their level of ineffi-ciency (Barsh 1977).[4]

Over the next three decades, all segments of the fishery continued to expand. There were 191 purse seine licenses issued in 1939 and 452 in 1961. Gillnetters nearly doubled their numbers, from 450 in 1939 to 856 in 1961. The troll fleet had increased to 1,300 boats by 1951 and more than quadru-pled over the next 20 years (Netboy 1974, 352). The overcapitalization problem was severe—in addition to the usual open-access problems, can-neries offered incentive payments to fishermen, thereby encouraging new entrants and ensuring that relatively inefficient boats were more likely to remain in the fishery.

A study commissioned by the state legislature in 1963 demonstrated that all harvestable fish in the Puget Sound fishery could be caught by one-half to two-thirds of the presently licensed fishermen, at a savings of from $700,000 to $2,500,000 (Royce et al. 1963). The study had little practical effect, and state officials maintained its policy of granting a license to any-one who applied, while the fishery continued to grow by leaps and bounds. A moratorium on licenses was not instituted until 1973, by which time the number of boats turning out for any fishery opening had reached truly prodigious proportions. By resisting the obvious solution of license limita-tion and instead relying on time closures and ever more cumbersome gear restrictions, the state was endangering both fishermen and fish stocks.[5]

International Competition

The struggle to manage international competition over salmon has been an ever-present backdrop to regulatory efforts within the state. Sockeye and pinks are among the most valuable stocks available to fishermen in the Pacific Northwest. Most of these fish are of Canadian origin but pass through Puget Sound on their way to spawning grounds in the Fraser River, which empties into Howe Sound about 40 miles north of the U.S.-

---

4. As analyzed by Barsh, the mechanics of this transfer are as follows. In a situation of open access, new entrants will be attracted to the troll fishery, since it is here that fish can be intercepted before reaching purse seines or gill nets. As the capacity to take more fish increases in the offshore fishery, managers must either shorten the troll season or limit purse seiners, gillnetters, or both. The state opted to limit purse seiners, which allowed the troll fishery to expand unchecked. Nor were any limits placed on the growing numbers of recre-ational fishermen (Barsh 1977).

5. One of the canons of fisheries management is to spread the catch effort over the entire period during which fish of a particular run are expected to be in an area. This policy is to ensure that no particular segment of the run is taken disproportionately by an intensive fishing effort.

Canadian border. During their migratory life cycle, these fish may pass in and out of U.S. and Canadian waters several times. A similar situation exists with respect to many of the Washington-origin coho and chinook. At various points along migratory routes, each side has opportunities to severely damage the stocks through overfishing. Without some sort of binding agreement, the temptation to engage in such "fish wars" is a constant threat. While all parties are aware of the advantages of cooperation and conservation, finding an agreement that both parties can accept is exceedingly difficult.

Discussions between U.S. and Canadian officials about the sharing of salmon stocks had been taking place since before the turn of the century, but little was accomplished prior to the 1930s.[6] Once the treaty was ratified in 1937, the United States and Canada were able to proceed with two important management objectives: (1) creating a joint regulatory commission to manage the stocks while they were in certain designated waters and (2) cooperating on a major fish restoration project in the Fraser River. Although the U.S.-Canadian treaty governing sockeye and pinks was ratified in 1937, other species were not covered until a new treaty was written in 1985 (and again, only after considerable delay and mutual threats to embark upon "fish wars"). The treaty contains a series of multiyear plans for fisheries on particular species. For a variety of reasons, it has become more difficult to negotiate new long-term plans as each of the existing plans has expired. Since 1992, fishing agreements are negotiated yearly, on a species-by-species basis, and it is not uncommon for the negotiation process to break down, as it did in 1997.

Recurrent Themes in State Management of Salmon

The history of the Puget Sound salmon fishery makes it clear that the roots of the problem and the pattern of state response to it were apparent early

---

6. The fact that a treaty was signed then may have been largely due to a misconception. The United States had been taking about two-thirds of the Fraser River runs throughout the early part of the century. Since it was unlikely that a treaty between the two countries would have given the United States a larger share of what were, arguably, Canadian stocks, the United States had something to lose and little to gain by negotiating. But in the 1936 season, immediately following the enactment of the Washington State initiative banning fish traps, Canadian fishermen caught 82 percent of the fish the treaty proposed to cover (Roos 1991, 47). It appears that the Americans believed that the two events were causally related; actually, it was more likely the result of a periodic change in the migratory path chosen by returning salmon—in 1936 the bulk of the run entered Howe Sound from the north, circumventing the U.S. fishing fleet almost entirely. In any case, the United States quickly altered its negotiating posture, and the same equal-sharing arrangement that had been proposed some six years earlier was accepted.

on and have remained constant throughout. The resource itself is a classic open-access resource with all of the associated collective action problems. To make matters worse, the value of each unit of the stock has remained consistently high, which has encouraged far more utilization than would be optimal, either in terms of the health of the resource itself or in terms of the amount of rent dissipation through overcapitalization. Salmon are highly migratory, so there are even fewer incentives than there would normally be for any particular fishermen or group of fishermen to conserve. And since the migratory path of salmon takes them across a number of regional, state, and international jurisdictions, there is diminished accountability for bureaucratic decision making.

It is not surprising, then, that several themes appear consistently under the state regulatory regime. The first is that, in general, state regulatory policy has been *reactive*—the state has done little to direct the development of the fishery; it has simply allowed it to develop naturally (and inefficiently, as fishing opportunities were continually being redistributed to groups that positioned themselves ahead of other groups). The state has limited its efforts to mitigating the effects of excessive fishing through time, place, and gear restrictions. In effect, conservation has been approached through mandating inefficiency, rather than limiting access. Another striking characteristic of state management is its emphasis on hatcheries. This emphasis is not hard to understand. Rather than confronting the problem of dividing a scarce resource between fishermen or, more important, between competing users of water and fish habitat such as residential developers, the timber industry, or the hydroelectric power industry, the state sought to augment the supply of fish while allowing competing economic development to proceed without interference. Not until the Northwest Power Planning Act was passed in 1980 was there an explicit directive that decisions about hydroelectric power development must consider the impact on salmon. And not until some Snake River and Columbia River stocks were listed under the Endangered Species Act has there been sustained, demonstrable concern about adverse impacts on wild, as opposed to hatchery, stocks.

The third characteristic is a consequence, no doubt partly unintended, of the first—regulation by inefficiency. Closing rivers to commercial fishing and issuing regulations that encourage fishing in marine areas had the effect, even if no discriminatory intent was present, of redistributing fishing opportunities from Indians to white fishermen. As fishing effort moves away from terminal to marine areas, it becomes less efficient not only because of biological considerations—fish are more dispersed, there is more mixing of stocks, and so on—but also because it requires more expensive gear. Indian fishermen have in the past been unable to finance entry into the purse seine or marine troll or gill net fisheries and so were systematically displaced. Their attempts to maintain traditional riverine fishery in the face of state "conservation" regulations that prohibited the use of nets in rivers made them obvious targets for public concerns about overfishing. This pattern of denial as to the real causes of problems in the salmon fishery and scapegoating of a readily identifiable group of "outsiders" is another recurrent theme.

U.S. v. Washington

Beginning in the late nineteenth century, Indians were pushed to the margins of the commercial fishery. Some tribal fishermen found jobs on boats owned by whites; most could not. Lack of capital or access to credit meant that few Indians could afford to buy the expensive boats necessary to enter the deepwater fishery. Some tribal members tried to fish commercially in traditional locations along rivers adjacent to the reservations, but this was contrary to state law and state fish and game officers seized gear and prosecuted fishermen who were caught. In the 1960s, Indian activists began to intensify efforts to establish and enforce tribal fishing rights. Influenced by the success of the black civil rights movement, they organized highly visible fishing in prohibited areas, such as the "fish-ins" that took place under the Puyallup River Bridge near the city of Tacoma, alongside a busy freeway in plain view of thousands of daily commuters. With the help of celebrities such as Marlon Brando and Dick Gregory, activists were successful in attracting national attention to the sometimes violent confrontations that ensued between tribal fishermen and state wardens or police officers.[7]

It was in this atmosphere of festering conflict that the United States, acting as trustee for seven Indian tribes, reluctantly brought suit against the State of Washington to obtain a legal determination of tribal fishing rights and have those rights enforced. Fourteen tribes later entered the case. *U.S. v. Washington* was not the first case to consider what rights had been guaranteed to Indians in the Stevens treaties, but it was the first in which it was the stated intention of the judge that this would be the broadest, most comprehensive adjudication of the issue surrounding treaty fishing rights to date.[8] The case was to take three and one-half years to

---

7. See Cohen 1986 for a more complete version of his highly conflictual and engrossing period in the development of tribal fishing rights in Washington state.

8. The decision in *U.S. v. Washington* (384 F. Supp. 312 [1974]) was not the "bolt of lightning" it was subsequently portrayed as. To anyone who examined the relevant cases immediately preceding it, particularly the combined cases of *U.S. v. Oregon* and *Sohappy v. Smith,* 302 F. Supp. 899 (1969), the handwriting was on the wall. See Cohen 1986 and Madson and Koss 1988 for accounts of the legal genealogy of *U.S. v. Washington.*

decide and involve voluminous reports by anthropologists, biologists, and other expert witnesses as well as lengthy testimony by state officials and tribal elders.

The basic questions to be resolved at trial were: What, if any, special fishing rights were guaranteed to the tribes by the treaties of 1854–55? Did such rights (if present) require allocation of the opportunity to catch a specific share of the resource? And if such rights were judged to be present, what was the extent of the State Department of Fisheries and the State Department of Game's management authority over their exercise? A second set of questions concerned (1) whether treaty rights to a particular share of the fish also conveyed the right to environmental protection of the habitat sustaining those fish and (2) whether treaty rights applied equally to fish reared in state-financed hatcheries. The latter set of questions was separated from issues of allocation and management authority and the two parts of *U.S. v. Washington* became known as Phase I and Phase II. Phase II did not receive a hearing until 1980. Phase I was decided in 1974, although considerable time elapsed before it was fully implemented.

The outcome of the case hinged on the legal interpretation of a key phrase, which appeared in all the treaties in nearly identical form. The treaties state that "the right of taking fish at all usual and accustomed grounds and stations is further secured to said Indians in common with all citizens of the United States" (Treaty of Point No Point 1855, cited in Cohen 1986). At trial, a range of interpretations was presented. The state had historically considered the phrase as conveying no rights to tribal members other than those extended to all state residents. One of the state agencies in charge of fisheries management, the Department of Game, continued to maintain this position. Both the Washington State Department of Fisheries and the United States held that the tribes were entitled to a particular share of the fishery, although they differed on what the appropriate share was. The tribes argued that at the time the treaties were signed, they had no intention of giving up ownership of what was their most valuable asset, and thus they were entitled to fish without restriction now.

On February 12, 1974, Judge Boldt ruled that treaty tribes were entitled to 50 per cent of the fish that passed through the "usual and accustomed" fishing areas of the tribes, plus whatever catch was needed for subsistence and ceremonial use. That was in addition to the treaty right to catch fish on the reservations, which no one had ever disputed. Washington state fishery officials were to manage nontreaty fishing in such a way as to allow treaty fishermen an opportunity to catch a 50 percent share of what would have passed through usual and accustomed places had it not been for prior interception by non-Indian fishermen in state waters and beyond—in effect, half of all salmon currently being managed by the state.

The process of defining where each tribe would be allowed to fish, what providing "opportunity to take" actually required, and how to compute the total harvestable share took a number of years to resolve.

The court sharply limited the state's authority to regulate tribal fishing. In order to restrict fishing by treaty tribes, the state had to show that regulations were "reasonable and necessary to prevent demonstrable harm to the actual conservation of the fish" and that alternatives, including restrictions on non-Indian fishing, had to have been exhausted (*U.S. v. Washington* 384 F.Supp. 312 [1974]). Thus, the state could no longer meet its conservation obligations by shutting down fisheries in terminal areas; it was now required to balance allocation and conservation throughout the succession of fisheries, from the coast to the rivers that drain into Puget Sound. Some state laws governing fishing, such as the designation of steelhead as a "game" fish (and thus off-limits to commercial net fishing) were deemed discriminatory and unnecessary.

The ruling was broad, far-reaching, and extremely controversial. Eventually, it would have the effect of profoundly altering the state-tribal relations with respect to a whole range of subjects, but the immediate reaction was quite different. Within the decision, Judge Boldt states his belief that

> the vast majority of the residents of this state . . . are fair, reasonable and law abiding people. They expect that kind of solution to all adjudicated controversies . . . and they will accept and abide by those decisions even if adverse to interests of their occupation or recreational activities. (*U.S. v. Washington,* 329)

The level of misplaced faith demonstrated by this statement is breathtaking in light of the political firestorm that subsequently ensued. The decision was assailed by newspaper editors across western Washington and by public officials in the state legislature and beyond. Judge Boldt himself was the target of protest demonstrations in which he was burned in effigy by irate fishermen. Bumper stickers stating "Can Boldt, Not Salmon" and similar sentiments emblazoned the vehicles of fishermen and their sympathizers. Judge Boldt, an elderly and politically conservative man, was accused of everything from believing in communism to being in the pay of large corporations to conducting an illicit sexual relationship with an Indian woman.

For the next four years, illegal fishing was widespread, and threats of violence against treaty fishermen and Washington Department of Fisheries enforcement officers were common. In 1978, a gillnetter was shot and paralyzed as a Washington State Department of Fisheries patrol attempted to arrest him for illegal fishing. Ironically, later studies showed that the main effect of altered fishing regulations during this period was to redistribute catch from commercial gillnetters and purse seiners to sport fishermen and trollers, not to treaty fishermen.

Considering that the commercial fishery was already severely overcrowded, it is not entirely surprising that nontreaty fishermen reacted with rage and frustration to a decision that required nontreaty fishing to be restricted in order to give Indian fishermen an opportunity to catch their share. The resistance did not end there, however. Officials at nearly every level of government supported the effort to thwart the court's decision. While the Washington State Department of Fisheries was alternately lackluster or recalcitrant in its implementation of the court's order, the Washington State Department of Game, which regulates steelhead fisheries, flatly refused to accept it. U.S. Senator Slade Gorton, who was then the state's attorney general, intensified the divisive atmosphere by publicly referring to Indians as "supercitizens" and encouraging opponents of the federal court's decision to believe it would ultimately be overturned (Cohen 1986, 90). Four years after the court's decision, the treaty share of fish was still only 17 per cent, yet the state's two senators were urging that full implementation of the ruling be further postponed (Washington State Department of Fisheries 1993). The International Salmon Commission steadfastly refused to make any alterations to accommodate the tiny Indian fleet and instead insisted that treaty fishermen be bound by the same time and gear regulations governing everyone else.[9]

A complete history of attempts to delay or thwart the federal court's decision will not be undertaken here, but by 1977, the conflict had reached an impasse. After reluctantly promulgating regulations designed to ensure the opportunity for the treaty tribes to take 50 percent of the harvestable fish, the Washington State Department of Fisheries was sued by various nontreaty user groups. The case went to the Washington State Supreme Court, which developed its own interpretation of rights conveyed by the Stevens treaties and then attempted to nullify the federal court's ruling by ordering the Department of Fisheries to cease enforcing regulations designed to divide fishing opportunity between treaty and nontreaty fishermen. At this point, the federal district court blocked the state court order and assumed direct management of the fishery itself. The federal district court's actions were upheld in 1978 by the U.S. Court of Appeals, which

---

9. In 1975, the Northwest Indian Fisheries Commission estimated that the total fleet size of all tribes having access to the area under the jurisdiction of the International Pacific Salmon Fisheries Commission was 65 large gillnet boats, 39 gillnet skiffs, and 4 purse seine boats. By contrast, the 1974 nontreaty fleet was 1,140 gillnet vessels, 54 reef nets, and 272 purse seines (cited in *U.S. v. Washington,* 459 F.Supp. 1020 [1978], 1051).

noted, "The state's extraordinary machinations in resisting the decree have forced the district court to take over a large share of the management of the state's fishery in order to enforce its decrees. Except for some desegregation cases [citations omitted] the district court has faced the most concerted official and private efforts to frustrate a decree of a federal court witnessed in this century" (*Puget Sound Gillnetters Association v. United States District Court*, 573 F.2d 1123 (1978), 1126 (9th Cir.).

The following year, over tribal objections, the Solicitor General of the United States agreed to Washington State's request for review of the case by the U.S. Supreme Court, which had already declined to review the decision in 1976. In 1979 the Supreme Court issued an opinion that upheld the original decision on all important issues, although it did limit the tribal share to 50 percent, including on-reservation catch and any catch used for subsistence and ceremonial purposes. The 50 percent allocation could be reduced only if the tribal members could be assured a "moderate living" with less than that amount. The state retained the authority to intervene in fisheries management (both on and off the reservation), but only when it could demonstrate a clear conservation interest (*Washington v. Passenger Fishing Vessel Association*, 443 U.S. 658 [1979]). The federal district court continued to oversee management of the fisheries, and it rarely found that the state met the required standard in demonstrating a conservation need.

Throughout the late 1970s and into early 1980, the state and the tribes had litigated nearly every aspect of fisheries management. The strain—on the tribes' side, of continually having to assert the rights it had been ensured by the treaties and by the courts, and on the state's side, of having to insulate every management decision from potential legal challenge—resulted, according to participants on both sides, in a lack of attentiveness to the overall health of the resource system. Beginning with the Supreme Court decision, a number of events intervened to disrupt this destructive pattern.

In 1980, Federal District Court Judge Orrick heard Phase II of *U.S. v. Washington* and ruled that a right to environmental protection was a necessary part of the tribes' right to one-half the harvestable fish.[10] In essence, then, the tribes had potential veto power over any major development that affected the habitat of salmon. The ruling was subsequently somewhat diluted by a higher court, but it nonetheless had the effect of strongly encouraging the state to embrace a less confrontational negotiat-

---

10. The legal ruling in *U.S. v. Washington* Phase II also established that hatchery fish were to be treated exactly the same as natural fish for the purposes of sharing between the tribes and the state. A tribal expert witness estimated the hatchery share of some species of Puget Sound salmon at at least 60 percent (testimony of Phil Mundy, cited in Cohen 1986, 213 n. 15).

ing position with respect to fisheries management. A series of meetings and retreats that became known as the Port Ludlow meetings are largely credited with providing the basis for mutual understanding that paved the way to a more cooperative management regime. In addition, at the urging of Senator Warren G. Magnuson, Congress passed the Salmon and Steelhead Conservation and Enhancement Act of 1980. The act provided $129 million to improve coordination between tribal, state, and federal managers of the fishery and to increase production through enhancement. The state increased the penalties for illegal fishing, and state courts began cooperating by enforcing the new penalties. And in 1981, the state's new governor replaced many high-ranking officials in the state departments of Fisheries and Game in an effort to build the basis for a more cooperative management regime. Through a combination of threats and rewards, the bureaucratic culture of the Department of Fisheries was substantially reoriented.[11]

The Current Regulatory Regime

The regulatory regime for each year's salmon fisheries is the outgrowth of a series of regional and international negotiation forums between representatives of different management agencies. Beginning in February with meetings between the United States and Canada, the tribes and the state regulatory agencies participate in a series of meetings in which the stocks are assessed and management options proposed, debated, and decided upon. The decisions reached at each forum define the management options for subsequent forums. Actors who share interests in one forum may oppose each other in another.

Pacific Salmon Commission

The process of allocating and regulating salmon harvests begins with the Pacific Salmon Commission (PSC), which was created as part of the U.S.-Canada Salmon Interception Treaty signed by the two nations in 1985. The commission sets quotas by species and region, which are then used as regulatory parameters by local jurisdictions. The treaty tribes, the state of Alaska, the states of Washington and Oregon together, and the federal government each have one representative on the PSC. All three nonfederal U.S. representatives must agree on decisions reached by the U.S. contingent. Doing so is often quite difficult because Alaska, whose fisheries are

---

11. Chapter 4 relates in more detail how this bureaucratic reorientation process was accomplished.

the first to intercept both Canadian and Washington or Oregon stocks, frequently has interests that sharply diverge from those of the other U.S. representatives. Nor is it unusual for there to be conflicts of interest within the tribal or state coalitions. On the Canadian side, there are also four commissioners. Collectively, each side has one vote.

The overarching principles guiding decision making by the PSC are (1) to prevent overfishing and (2) to assure that each side receives "benefits equivalent to the production of salmon originating in its waters" (Madson and Koss 1988, 13). The commission's three panels, Northern, Southern, and Fraser River, are charged with the responsibility of making policy recommendations consistent with those goals.[12] The panels consist of representatives of the treaty tribes, the federal government, and the states, and on two of the panels, a representative of either the commercial or sportfishing interests. Regulatory policy recommended by the Northern and Southern panels are advisory only and are meant to be implemented by the provincial, state, federal, or tribal regulatory agencies. The Fraser River Panel, which regulates the large and highly lucrative Fraser River sockeye fishery along the Straits of Juan de Fuca and the San Juan Islands on the U.S. side, actually carries out day-to-day fishery management.

The Pacific Fishery Management Council

The Fishery Conservation and Management Act of 1976 created eight regional councils to regulate fisheries conducted in the zones 3 to 200 miles off U.S. coastlines. In February and March of each year, the Pacific Fishery Management Council (PFMC) begins to draft a management plan for ocean fisheries in California, Oregon, and Washington. The PFMC has 13 voting members, including the regional director of the National Marine Fisheries Service, representatives of the state fisheries departments of Washington, Oregon, California, and Idaho, and 8 private citizens chosen by the U.S. Secretary of Commerce from lists prepared by the governors of each state. In recent years, the governor of Washington has always included a tribal representative.

In a series of public meetings and private negotiating sessions with user groups, the PFMC investigates various regulatory options and attempts to balance allocation between sportfishing and commercial groups and treaty and nontreaty fishermen. In determining the share of fish that can be taken in the ocean, the PFMC is also determining what share will be left for the "inside" fisheries (those inside Puget Sound), and

---

12. One immediate effect of the 1985 treaty has been to significantly reduce the proportion of Fraser River sockeye taken by U.S. fishermen.

negotiations among all these groups are intense and often conflictual. The PFMC must also manage the fishery in accordance with the biological needs of the various species, which involves taking into account the inter-relationships between various strong and weak stocks, setting escapement goals, and drafting time, place, and gear requirements. Along the Washington coast, the PFMC is legally required to allocate fish on a species-by-species, river system–by–river system basis to ensure that each tribe receives fishing opportunities.

The State of Washington and the Tribes

During and after the PFMC's determination of the regulatory regime that will govern the ocean fisheries, the tribes and the Washington Departments of Fish and Wildlife negotiate and then adopt a plan to manage fisheries in the remaining areas—within three miles of the Washington coast, the Straits of Juan de Fuca, Puget Sound, and the state's rivers. The same process of establishing and implementing biological requirements while allocating between competing user groups is played out once more, although the structure of authority is more complicated at this level. Since the fishing rights of any tribe are place-bound, decisions about when and where the harvestable portion of a given run will be taken affect different tribes differently. Rather than negotiating with the tribes as a block, the state must conduct simultaneous bilateral negotiations with representatives from the various subsets of tribes sharing particular river systems. The tribes as well must negotiate among themselves about regulations for shared and in-common areas. All decisions must be made by consensus, which results in protracted negotiations. State-tribal and intertribal relations, of which these negotiations are a large part, are discussed in chapters 4 and 5.

To recapitulate, every year the regulatory bodies go through a series of steps in different negotiating forums in order to arrive at the regulations that will govern individual fishermen. First, in early February, representatives of the states, the federal government, the treaty tribes, and Canada work out fishing regulations in accordance with preestablished goals and quotas. In March and April, the Pacific Fishery Management Council—a regional council comprised of government fishery officials and representatives of user-groups—develops a management plan for the fisheries conducted from 3 to 200 miles off the U.S. coast. In so doing, they unavoidably set the parameters of the subsequent fisheries inside Puget Sound and within 3 miles of the coast. Next, the state and the tribes must work out a plan to coordinate their joint utilization of the resource. Finally, individual tribes develop regulations for their own fishermen and the state develops regulations for the nontreaty fishery. Beneath the surface of the negotiations taking place at each step of this process are patterns of divergent interests that continually strain relations between members of state, tribal and national coalitions.

Conclusion

This chapter has discussed the historical development of the fishery, the legal decision that was the driving force behind the implementation of comanagement, and the current process of decision making that governs regulation of the salmon fishery. I have begun to demonstrate some of the difficulties and enormous complexity involved in managing this resource. A number of factors account for this complexity. First, salmon are a highly migratory resource, which cross and recross international boundaries and political jurisdictions. They are harvested by a large number of heterogeneous user groups, which have great difficulty in reaching comprehensive management agreements. Fish habitat is highly vulnerable to incompatible uses of water resources by power companies, farmers, and logging companies, which further undercuts the incentives for any particular subgroup to exercise self-restraint in fishing. There is a recent history of huge political controversy and turmoil surrounding rights to utilize this resource, and a longer history of weak regulatory controls and scapegoating of Indians for the failures of state policies. The elucidation of these factors is intended to provide the background for the subsequent evolution of comanagement institutions.

CHAPTER 4

Institutions of Comanagement

The effect of the court's ruling in *U.S. v. Washington* was to redefine property rights to a large, complex resource system. The new property rights necessitated the creation of new institutions to govern what was now a shared management responsibility. While the court had ordered that the parties cooperate, it did not (nor could it) specify the best way to accomplish that end. The state regulatory agencies and the tribes themselves were faced with the task of solving the various collective action problems involved in creating successful governance structures.

This chapter begins with a description of the sources of the transaction costs involved in creating comanagement institutions. Some of these were onetime costs; others are ongoing. Some were directly attributable to the history of poor relations between the two sets of actors. Others are intrinsic to the underlying pattern of the parties' often conflicting interests and could be expected to exist in any such collaborative effort. I next discuss the institutions currently governing the three areas of salmon management where state agencies and tribes interact. In areas where the underlying interests of the two sides are reasonably consonant—hatchery production and habitat preservation—the evolution of new institutions was rapid once certain key questions were settled, and the current institutions appear stable and relatively efficient. In the area of harvest management, where the two sets of actors have strong competing interests, the pace of change has been slower and the current institutions continue to reflect the high transaction costs of allocating a scarce resource in a situation where there is considerable uncertainty and thus many areas for strategic action. At the same time, these institutions are a quantum leap forward from the institutions that preceded them with respect to the mitigation of such transaction costs. Finally, I assess some of the distinctive features of the institutions governing tribal-state collaboration and discuss how comanagement has altered the traditional style of salmon management in this state.

What becomes apparent is that over time, these two sets of actors have been able to design institutions that are more effective in reducing the transaction costs involved in their collaboration than those devised by a centralized political authority such as the federal court. The history of rancor between the two sides would suggest that their interactions should be rigidly bound by formal rules and court-imposed structures. Yet in practice, the parties rely largely on informal institutions that they themselves have developed to structure their interactions, and in these, there is considerable departure from formal rules and a surprising degree of mutual accommodation and recognition of each other's interests.

The Beginning of Comanagement

The obstacles to creating a successful comanagement system were formidable, as the previous account of post-Boldt relations between the tribes and the state suggests. Consider search costs. Even seemingly straightforward search activities such as establishing the identities and preferences of the relevant parties were complicated. This process was not helped by several changes in the set of players: for example, the original 14 tribes were eventually joined by seven others; under provisions of the 1976 Fishery Conservation and Management Act, the newly created Pacific Fishery Management Council (PFMC) began managing the ocean fisheries from 3 to 200 miles off the Washington, Oregon, and California coasts; and the 1985 Pacific Salmon Treaty between the United States and Canada introduced several substantially reconfigured regulatory commissions, which for the first time included tribal representatives. Other types of search costs involved reaching agreement on the data and models to be used in generating the numbers of harvestable fish and were also high.[1]

Although it might appear that the court's designation of a 50–50 allocational split lowered bargaining costs, they remained extraordinarily high because the state (and a large segment of the public) was unwilling to accept the legal decision. While the ruling was being challenged through legislative and legal channels, it probably appeared far from certain that it would continue to be law. This uncertainty compromised whatever incentives there were to begin the process of constructing viable institutions of comanagement. Once it had been upheld by the Supreme Court in 1979, that uncertainty was settled, but there were still a number of unresolved technical questions, such as how and where fish were to be counted. Much of the information necessary to carry out what had become a far more complicated management responsibility simply was not available. In addition, there is a great deal of scientific uncertainty inherent in salmon man-

---

1. According to a former director of the Washington Department of Fisheries, in the early 1980s it was common for the state and the tribes to go to court over exceedingly minor differences in biological predictions (Turner interview 1993).

agement that creates any number of margins that one side or the other can attempt to bias in its favor and thus increase the costs of bargaining.[2]

Enforcement costs, particularly in the 1974–79 period, were extremely high, far beyond the capacity of the system to meet them. Wholesale illegal fishing occurred among nontreaty fishermen, motivated by both protest and opportunism. Illegal fishing by nontreaty fishermen was used as a justification by treaty fishermen for their own illegal fishing. Added to that was the perception that large numbers of nontreaty fishermen were fishing illegally and the state appeared either unwilling or unable to do much about it. Tribal courts and legal codes were still fairly undeveloped, and state courts frequently refused to punish illegal fishing by nontreaty fishermen.[3]

In short, the parties faced very high transaction costs, which made the creation of successful, efficient governance structures exceedingly difficult. The high information costs that are part and parcel of the management of a large, complex transboundary resource system about which there is a great deal of scientific uncertainty readily lent themselves to both the perception and the reality of advantage seeking on either side. In addition, state agencies strongly resisted relinquishing their traditional hegemony.[4] The immediate result was that throughout the 1970s, the two sides litigated nearly every management decision made by the other, and formal disputes alone numbered in the hundreds every year. Enormous amounts of staff time were consumed in preparing and presenting justifications in court for decisions that often represented fairly trivial differences. This pattern continued for seven or eight years after the legal ruling. Neither side seemed willing to compromise, although the process was highly costly to both.

Conflicts typically played out in the following way. One or more tribes would issue regulations opening an area to tribal fishermen, which would then be challenged by the state, usually on the grounds that it threatened conservation goals. Some tribal fishermen would proceed to fish anyway, whereupon state enforcement officers would cite them, often seizing their gear at the same time. In the meantime, the federal district

---

2. One tribal fisheries manager refers to the dynamics of negotiating in the context of scientific uncertainty as the problem of "dueling biologists" and claims that if "you put 10 different biologists in a room, you are going to get 10 different answers, and politics will pick the answer" (Troutt interview 1993).

3. In their pleadings before the U.S. Supreme Court, the tribes noted that in only one of 300 citations issued to non-Indian fishermen in 1975 was a penalty issued. Brief of Respondent Indian Tribes, *State of Washington v. Washington State Commercial Passenger Fishing Vessel Association and Washington Kelpers Association,* U.S. (1978), 65, n. 231, 232 (cited in Cohen 1986, 204 n. 22).

4. For state managers, the allocation issues involved in ceding 50 percent of the harvest to the tribes were less problematic than ceding a large part of its regulatory authority.

court, which by then was spending inordinate amounts of time overseeing the fisheries, would hear the dispute and, more often than not, conclude that the state had not met the admittedly high burden of proof that required that state biologists exhaust other means of meeting escapement goals before forcing the conservation burden onto the Indian fisheries.

Since the mid-1980s, there has been a dramatic turnaround in state-tribal relations. Near-total reliance on formal rules laid down by the court—what some have derisively but accurately called "management by court order"—has given way to the current system of cooperative management through jointly created management plans and projects. There is relatively open communication between the two sides and face-to-face negotiations with little need for recourse to the court for adjudication or enforcement of formal and informal rules. While points of friction and distrust remain, representatives of the two sides generally speak of having a good working relationship with each other and do in fact collaborate on projects of mutual interest. Given the history of bitter relations between the two sides, the transformation is remarkable, and it has taken place in a relatively short period of time.

It was not, by and large, a process in which both sides made significant compromises and gradually came to occupy a middle ground. The position of the tribes changed very little: throughout this period they had demanded their full allocational share and the right to exercise management authority over their fisheries and over decisions that directly affected their fisheries. State managers, on the other hand, substantially altered their decision-making rules and procedures as the bureaucratic culture of the organization was changed from above. Although a number of factors were important in explaining this process of transformation, the role of political leadership proved to be crucial.

Beginning in the early 1980s, the state initiated a process of rapprochement during which it signaled its willingness to cooperate with the tribes.[5] Several factors appear to have prompted this change. First, the state had amassed a stunning record of defeats in court, and its prospects for regaining its traditional position of preeminent authority seemed increasingly dim. Second, the regulatory disarray that had characterized the middle and late 1970s was clearly taking a toll on the resource system, which created the perception on both sides that Solomonic judgments were called for. Third, formal negotiations between the United States and

---

5. Many observers distinguish between the "comanagement" period, in which the two sides basically engaged in unilateral decision making and frequently were challenged by their counterparts, and "cooperative" management, which is distinguished by joint decision making (Pattillo interview 1992).

Canada over salmon allocation were at a standoff, and steadily escalating "fish wars" between the parties were a cause for concern among both commercial and recreational non-Indian fishers. The state of Alaska was the key holdout, and the tribes had leverage that could bring that state's delegation to the negotiating table.[6] Perhaps most important, in 1980 the tribes won a broad, albeit ill-defined, right to environmental protection of fish habitat, a decision that sent shock waves throughout the state government and the business community. The generally accepted view among political and corporate leaders was that negotiation and compromise over fisheries management were preferable to the risks of continued litigation in the much broader area of environmental protection.[7]

The fact that creating a more cooperative relationship between the tribes and the state was rational from the state's perspective does not in itself explain either why or how it came to be. Initially, there were few incentives to dissuade state fisheries biologists from resisting any accommodation with the tribes.[8] This situation changed in 1981 when the state's newly elected governor appointed a new director to the Washington State Department of Fisheries. The new director, who was not a scientist but an attorney, is credited with a series of far-reaching internal changes, many of which were initially strongly resisted. Staff members were strongly encouraged to reach cooperative agreements with the tribes, and authority in the

---

6. The tribes had quite credibly threatened to pursue an attempt to have their treaty rights to one-half the harvestable salmon extended into the Alaskan fisheries. In exchange for the Alaskan delegation's agreement to sign the Pacific Salmon Treaty, the tribes agreed not to pursue such litigation for the lifetime of the treaty. Since Alaska had the power to block the treaty, and without a treaty the Canadians could have caught whatever additional fish the tribes might have obtained through a favorable court ruling, it was probably a rational strategy. In addition, the Pacific Salmon Treaty provides for formal representation of the treaty tribes on par with U.S. and state representatives. See Yanagida 1987 for more details on the negotiation of the 1985 Pacific Salmon Treaty.

7. After the Phase II decision, attorney James Waldo, who had formerly represented the tribes in court and was a member of the federal task force set up in 1977 to resolve the controversy, was hired by a number of large corporations as a consultant. Reasoning that either litigation or an effort to pass defensive legislation was risky and expensive, Waldo recommended mediated negotiations with the tribes on specific issues, together with support for greater tribal recognition and participation in government decision making (Waldo 1981). Because of his prior experience with all the relevant parties, Waldo was able to act as a political entrepreneur in reducing the transaction costs to any of the parties of establishing each other's preferences and beliefs about the other.

8. As noted in chapter 1, many policy analysts and professional resource managers believe that users of a resource are virtually incapable of managing a resource system in a sustainable fashion because of the presence of what they would describe as inherent conflicts of interest. Thus, fisheries managers tend to adopt a view of their roles as protecting a resource against the "predations" of user groups. In this case, the fact that these user groups were Indian fishermen seems to have exacerbated the situation for some state biologists.

department became more centralized. Fisheries biologists were ordered to resolve technical disputes at levels where they arose, rather than allowing them to become policy or legal disputes. Doing so greatly increased the amount of direct communication between state and tribal fisheries biologists, whose previous interaction had been largely through their respective attorneys or in a formal dispute-resolution process set up by the court. In addition, career advancement for state Fisheries Department employees became linked with success in reaching agreements with the tribes. Ultimately, six of eight occupants of key positions within the department were replaced or left voluntarily (Pinkerton and Keitlah 1990). The process of reorienting its own rules, practices and bureaucratic culture was a major preoccupation in the Washington State Department of Fisheries from 1983–87 (Turner interview 1993).

While the Washington State Department of Fisheries was being changed from within, the new director initiated a series of face-to-face meetings and retreats with tribal leaders, biologists, and policymakers and their counterparts at the Washington State Department of Fisheries. Known as the Port Ludlow meetings after the retreat where they took place, they are cited by nearly all observers as a critical turning point in state-tribal relations. In addition to providing a forum in which the parties were forced to actually discuss their differences, these meetings appear to have been important symbolically in convincing the tribes that state managers were willing to recognize them as legitimate bargaining partners. And by establishing some minimal level of common ground, they seem to have made it possible for the two sides to begin to work together on projects where they had common adversaries. For example, in 1986, several tribes and the state joined in a legal action designed to protect fish habitat against incursions from the Army Corps of Engineers. Thus, while the process of transforming the organization was initiated from above, somewhat coercively, it became at least partly self-generating as fisheries biologists and policy analysts on each side came to recognize that they had some areas of common interest where they were potential allies. This artful blend of carrots and sticks has ultimately resulted in the development of a foundation of functional institutions with at least a modicum of mutual trust.[9]

---

9. The relatively low levels of conflict between the parties today is doubtless partly attributable to the fact that the proportion of staff members who did not directly experience the period of high-conflict years of the 1970s and 1980s grows larger every year. In addition, the number of women in staff positions has steadily increased, a fact that at least one key observer views as significant in explaining the more cooperative character of the system today (Pauley interview 1996).

Institutions of Comanagement

Habitat Management and Hatchery Production

State agencies and the tribes have a common interest in restoring and protecting fish habitat. The deterioration of habitat is one of the major limiting factors on the supply of many stocks of salmon, and restoring or at
least curtailing the loss of fish habitat is key to expanding the supply of
fish. Increasing the number of harvestable fish makes possible a Pareto-
superior solution to many of the conflicts over allocation facing the tribes
and the state. While the benefits of preserving and restoring fish habitat are
enjoyed by both sides, the burden of costs is borne largely by the state or
private interests. Since the tribes would not normally share directly in
benefits derived from competing uses of fish habitat such as residential
growth, development of hydroelectric power, or logging, their costs in
seeking to protect or rehabilitate fish habitat are limited to those incurred
in bargaining with other user groups and the costs involved in physically
restoring streams.

While the state resource agencies also have a strong stake in conserving fish habitat, their interests are far more nuanced. State agencies are
accountable to the state legislature, which is subject to pressure by a variety of interests, many of which favor present use patterns of water
resources. For the state as a whole, preserving and rehabilitating fish habitat represents significant opportunity costs.

As a result of decisions reached in Phase II of *U.S. v. Washington,* the
tribes have a legal right to environmental protection of the salmon
resource, although the status of this right remains undefined.[10] In the
minds of state officials, the possibility of tribal litigation that would establish a federally protected right to issue of environmental protection
remains a very real one (Turner interview 1993). For the state and for private interests, this is a situation of ongoing uncertainty wherein the tribes
could challenge particular development projects at any time.

---

10. Reasoning that a 50 percent allocation right necessarily required a right to environmental protection of the resource, Phase II of *U.S. v. Washington* was originally decided in
the tribes' favor. The state appealed, and after a series of confusing decisions, the Ninth Circuit Court of Appeals ultimately ruled that while an unqualified environmental right could
not be established, the tribes could be entitled to environmental protections in certain specific
cases. So far, the treaty right has been used to either block construction of or alter the operation of dams (*Confederated Tribes of the Umatilla v. Alexander,* 440 F.Supp.553 [1985], and
Kittitas Reclamation Dist. v. Sunnyside Valley Irrigation Dist., 763 F .2d 1032, [9th Cir. 1985])
and stop construction of a marina (*Muckleshoot Indian Tribe v. Hall,* 698 F. Supp. 1504, 1516
[W.D. Wash. 1988]). See Natural Resources Law Institute 1990,8–19 for more details.

The state's strategy for dealing with this uncertainty has had two elements. First, the state legislature has committed funds to enhancement (fish hatcheries) and the restoration of habitat. In 1986, the tribes and the state participated in the Watershed Planning Process in which subregional teams of representatives from the Washington state departments of Fisheries and Wildlife and the tribes developed lists of key areas in need of habitat restoration or areas where there were opportunities to enhance salmon production. From those lists, the Washington State Department of Fisheries developed a proposal that eventually received about $4 million from the Legislature for the 1987–89 biennium.

Second, the tribes have been included in a number of newly created decision-making forums regarding land-use and water-use planning. The prototype of these is the Timber/Fish/Wildlife Agreement, which grew out of a series of meetings between representatives of the tribes, the timber industry, environmental organizations, and state government. The agreement was intended to forestall litigation, particularly litigation related to forestry practices that were considered to have a detrimental effect on salmon streams. Under the Timber/Fish/ Wildlife Agreement, representatives from the tribes, the state agencies, the timber industry, and environmentalists sit on a board that reviews applications for logging contracts and related forestry work, monitors compliance with environmental laws, and collects data for a variety of wildlife habitat projects and water quality and associated projects. With Bureau of Indian Affairs funding, the tribes have been able to develop a number of projects rehabilitating local streams, gathering data, and monitoring timber contracts.[11]

In 1989, the tribes and the state signed an Environmental Memorandum of Understanding formalizing the set of principles for joint decision making between the tribes and the state that have evolved over the years and pledging further cooperative efforts. The document states that while both sides "recognize the potential for litigation in either the general or specific case, . . . the parties have learned that the benefits of cooperative resolution of disputes may exceed those obtainable through litigation" (Northwest Indian Fisheries Commission n.d., 38). While the Memorandum of Understanding is not legally binding, it has been cited in recent agreements between the tribes and the state, such as the Chelan Agreement of 1990. The Chelan Agreement attempts to apply the principle of cooperative decision making and compromise to the allocation of water

11. During fiscal years 1988–91, the state contributed approximately $15 million to Timber/Fish/Wildlife projects, the environmental organizations contributed $350,000, and the tribes received funding from the Bureau of Indian Affairs of $2 million per year, which was shared among the tribes and an intertribal organization, the Northwest Indian Fisheries Commission (Northwest Indian Fisheries Commission n.d.).

resources. It resulted from a series of meetings between tribal representatives, state officials, representatives of agricultural interests, hydroelectric power interests, commercial fishing interests, and environmental groups—several hundred individuals in all. The lead agency in one of two pilot projects initiated under the Chelan Agreement is the Jamestown S'Klallam Tribe (Seiter interview 1993).

Increased cooperation between the tribes and the state as expressed in the Timber/Fish/Wildlife Agreement and similar agreements has generated both praise and criticism. While opinions vary whether such institutions serve the public interest, it is clear that the tribes and the state have at least partially succeeded in carrying out an agenda that they perceive is in their collective best interests.[12] Among other things, these agreements have resulted in substantial funds being pumped into tribal and state governments through the creation of new staff positions.

At the level of planning and day-to-day operations, state personnel in the habitat division of the Washington State Department of Fisheries and their counterparts employed by the tribes generally work together well. As one state habitat manager puts it, "Habitat is like a motherhood-and-apple-pie issue—nobody is going to argue that you shouldn't have habitat. So it's real easy to get your heads together and protect something you know is a good thing" (Sekulich interview 1993). Several divisions within the habitat section of the Department of Fisheries work on enhancement opportunities such as potential spawning and rearing streams that are for some reason inaccessible to salmon. Many of these potential projects have been previously identified during stream surveys conducted by both the tribes and the state. Others were highlighted during the Watershed Planning Process.

Producing fish through fish hatcheries presents few of the trade-offs presented by habitat protection. With funds from state general revenues and the federal government, and mitigation funds from producers of hydroelectric power or other projects with negative impacts on fish, the Washington State Department of Fisheries has developed a large hatchery program. Many of the tribes also operate hatcheries, which make a significant contribution to overall fish production. Once the young fish leave the hatchery, they become part of the common pool to be allocated according to the 50–50 allocation rule. Nonetheless, it is only rarely the case that enhancement issues generate the same level of conflict as do harvest management decisions. In both habitat management and enhance-

---

12. See Halpert and Lee 1990 for a positive review of the Timber/Fish/Wildlife Agreement and the model of decision making it typifies; see Fraidenburg 1989 for a perspective that is strongly critical.

ment, the division of labor between the comanagers is relatively efficient, and the evolution of cooperative institutions has been rapid.

Harvest Management

Harvest management concerns allocation—deciding when, where, and how to divide the fish—and conservation—regulating the time, place, and manner of fishing in such as way as to ensure the maintenance of future runs. The interests of the parties clearly compete in such areas, and it is not surprising that harvest management is the most conflictual and difficult aspect of comanagement. The basic principles of harvest management as ordered by Judge Boldt are deceptively simple: the parties are to estimate the number of fish of each species returning to spawn; subtract the number necessary for escapement; and divide up the remaining harvestable fish, which each side can harvest using any combination of regulations it likes. In practice, however, this is an exceedingly complex process, fraught with uncertainty and opportunities for real or imagined advantage on either side. For example, Washington-origin fish travel several thousand miles on their way back to natal streams. When and where are they to be counted?

Competition between treaty and nontreaty fishermen involves both spatial and temporal dimensions. As the fish return to spawn, they pass through a succession of fisheries, each of which must be limited in order to allow enough fish for escapement and for subsequent fisheries. The recreational and commercial ocean fleets are the first to intercept the fish, and they are almost entirely non-Indian. Next are the commercial net fisheries in the marine waters inside Puget Sound, which are somewhat more mixed between treaty and nontreaty, but in which nontreaty fishermen predominate. The majority of tribal fishermen fish in the bays, river mouths, and rivers adjacent to their reservations.[13] Thus the composition of the fishing fleet changes from predominantly nontribal to predominantly tribal as the fish move from the ocean and the Straits of Juan de Fuca through Puget Sound and into the rivers—and as the fishing season progresses. One consequence is that the tribes can be counted upon to raise conservation issues early in the season when most of the fishing is taking place in the ocean, and the state will play a similar role late in the season as the fish move through Puget Sound and into the rivers, when the fisheries at issue are increasingly tribal.

To further complicate matters, both the tribes and the state have heterogeneous interests within their own coalitions. The state must balance

---

13. Although it is also true that the lion's share of the treaty share is taken in marine waters of Puget Sound, by the minority of treaty fishermen with large, powerful gillnet or purse seine boats.

the needs of recreational fishers, both in the marine waters and in the rivers, as well as those of commercial fishermen, both ocean trollers and net fishermen inside Puget Sound. The rivalry between these groups has been intense in recent years. Few treaty fishermen fish for recreation, but each tribe is limited to fishing within particular geographical locations, called "usual and accustomed places" (UAPs) that roughly correspond to where their ancestors fished. Decisions regarding conservation and when and where the treaty and nontreaty share will be taken have distributional consequences not only for the two sides relative to each other, but for different interests within each coalition.[14] Thus, a variety of issues having to do with biology and fisheries management get played out against a morass of distributional issues. This situation can be illustrated with a brief discussion of salmon ecology and how the management process works.[15]

Salmon Management

Six species of salmon and steelhead return to spawn in the rivers and tributaries of Puget Sound and the Washington coast: *Oncorhynchus tshawytscha* (chinook or king), *Oncorhynchus nerka* (sockeye or red), *Oncorhynchus gorbuscha* (pink, which only appear in alternate years), *Oncorhynchus kisutch* (coho or silver), *Oncorhynchus keta* (chum or dog), and *Salmo gairdneri* (steelhead). Each species is composed of a number of stocks—genetically distinct populations that home to a particular stream. For management purposes, these small stocks are lumped together by river system or in some cases by combining several small rivers or tributaries. Escapement goals are established for each natural stock and set the parameters for harvest decisions. Taken together, all stocks of a particular species comprise a run.

Different runs pass through different areas in successive but overlapping waves. Chinook begin entering Puget Sound in early spring, followed by sockeye and pinks in the summer months, and coho and chum in autumn and early winter. Sockeye salmon, pink salmon, and coho runs are usually fairly concentrated, moving through successive fisheries from the entrance to Puget Sound to their spawning grounds in the rivers in one to two months. Chinook and some chum appear in several waves and for management purposes are divided into early, middle, and late runs. The fishing season is divided into management periods, which correspond to the intervals during which the majority of a run (defined as 80 per cent) is expected to pass through a given area. Time and gear requirements are

---

14. Intertribal conflicts are the subject of chapter 5.

15. See W. Clark 1985, upon which this explanation draws, for a more complete rendition of the complexities of salmon management in this area.

keyed to the escapement goals of particular stocks present and change throughout the season, according to which runs are present in a particular area at a particular time. For all species, fisheries managers attempt to spread the catch throughout the run, in order to avoid altering the genetic pool by artificially selecting the early or late segment of the run.

Preliminary run estimates are used in coming up with the management plans negotiated between the state and the tribes prior to the season. Once the fishing season actually begins, the estimates are updated when the fish begin to near terminal areas. For the commercial fisheries, such updates are done with the help of information generated in test fisheries, update fisheries, and through the tickets detailing catch information that fish buyers must submit daily. By comparing these estimated catch figures with the prior predictions of run sizes, managers can determine whether their earlier predictions were accurate. This accounting system is used by both the state and the tribes to see whether escapement goals are going to be met and to keep track of how many fish have been caught in preceding fisheries and by whom, in order to calculate each side's remaining allocational share. Toward the end of the season, catch data are generated on a daily basis, as each side tries to catch its remaining share without fishing into the escapement.

Estimating recreational catches is more difficult, since there is less certainty about when and whether recreational fishermen send in the punch cards that the state uses to estimate overall sport catches. It is also much more difficult to predict how many fishermen will participate in an opening. Sportfishing has been an area of persistent disagreement between the two sides, since the tribes contend that the state consistently underestimates the recreational catch. During the negotiations prior to the 1992 season, one group of tribes insisted that the state undertake a costly survey for one segment of the recreational fishery, a survey which did in fact demonstrate that the recreational catch was much higher than anticipated.[16] The state was subsequently forced to close the recreational fishery in that region midway through the season.

All areas are closed to fishing unless specifically opened by either the state (for the nontreaty fishermen) or the tribes (for the treaty fishermen). While the jointly authored management plans set the management periods for the different stocks and lay out some general parameters for management, the actual fishing times and gear requirements are set for the respec-

---

16. On the other hand, a recently completed tribal-state study of the methods and techniques used to produce sport salmon catch estimates found that the state had been *overestimating* sport catches in all areas except Sekiu (the area mentioned above) by a factor of 20 percent in some areas and up to 46 percent in others (Washington State Department of Fisheries 1991).

tive groups by their respective regulatory agencies. Either side may challenge the regulations of the other on the basis of either conservation (if either side believes further fishing will compromise escapement goals) or allocation (if one side suspects the other has already taken its allocation). Where the tribes share usual and accustomed areas (and that is the rule, rather than the exception), each tribe has the authority to draft regulations for its own members, although the tribes make an effort to coordinate their regulations in shared areas. These regulations are updated weekly, guided by run size estimates and by how much of the two sides' allocational shares remain. Thus, in any one of the 32 designated fishing areas, there could conceivably be fishermen from perhaps seven tribes, plus the nontreaty fleet, all fishing under separate regulations that are updated on a weekly basis.

A number of additional factors complicate the management process. First, runs overlap, which results in conflicts between the requirements of various species. Particularly when the run of a weak stock of one species overlaps into the season of strong stocks of another species, this overlap creates difficulties. For example, Hood Canal wild coho has been a weak stock that has at times fallen short of making its escapement goal even when there is no fishery directed toward it. Normally, most Hood Canal wild coho make their way into freshwater spawning streams by the time the chum management period begins, but in low water conditions, they linger in salt-water areas, and their presence overlaps with that of the normally abundant Hood Canal chum. To fully protect the weak run, fisheries managers would have to delay the chum fishery until all coho have cleared the area, because it is impossible to catch chum without catching some coho. Delaying the opening may mean that fishermen are prevented from catching harvestable chum, a situation fisheries managers are understandably reluctant to bring about.

A similar problem comes up with respect to the many stocks in Puget Sound that have both a hatchery component and a natural component, whose biological requirements are not consistent with one another. Hatchery runs require only about a 10 per cent escapement, whereas even for healthy natural runs, the requirement is approximately 50 per cent. For a weak or depressed natural run, there may be *no* harvestable fish. If both runs are present simultaneously, fishery managers must choose between managing for the wild run, which results in wasting part of the hatchery run, or managing for the hatchery run, which damages the productivity of the natural run.

One of the most difficult aspects of managing Pacific salmon fisheries is the problem of mixed stocks. When fish are in the ocean prior to entering the Sound, dozens of stocks are mixed together and fishing is fairly indiscriminate across both stocks and age groups. The level of harvest that can be sustained by healthy stocks far outstrips that of weak stocks, and even if the weak stocks make up a very small percentage of the total numbers of fish present, some of their number will be caught incidentally. To ensure that enough of the weak stock return to their rivers of origin to spawn, fishing on other stocks must be constrained, often quite drastically.

While most biologists subscribe to the idea of protecting weak natural stocks whenever possible, the tribes have a special interest in establishing this as a primary principle of management. In the early 1980s, three north coastal tribes brought suit against the Pacific Fisheries Management Council (PFMC), which sets regulations for the ocean fisheries.[17] Previously, the PFMC had developed plans for treaty-nontreaty allocational shares based on species-by-species aggregation. This system left some coastal rivers and the tribes that fished almost entirely on those rivers without any harvestable fish. The federal court required that shares be balanced on a river-by-river, run-by-run basis.

The principle of weak-stock management—drafting regulations in such a way as to protect the weakest stock—has the effect of forcing a conservative regulatory regime, particularly on the ocean fisheries where the protection of one or more weak stocks necessitates forgoing the opportunity to harvest some fish from perhaps 40 to 50 strong stocks. As the fish move through Puget Sound and into the terminal areas, they separate into more-or-less discrete stocks, and it becomes possible for fishing regulations to discriminate more carefully between them. Weak-stock management in effect throws up a protective shield around the fish until they reach the terminal areas. That is an attractive proposition for many of the tribes because (1) they have only limited ocean fisheries and thus sacrifice little when ocean fishing is constrained, and (2) their major fishing areas are at or near the terminal areas, where they may be able to take advantage of any excess fish that have received protection incidental to the protection of a weak stock.

Treaty fisheries do share some of the burden of conservation under weak-stock management, so it is not an entirely costless strategy. For example, once the tribes have lobbied for weak-stock protection early on in the season during the PFMC meetings that set quotas for the ocean fisheries, their reputations and bargaining power in future negotiations are adversely affected if they subsequently take steps that erode or are inconsistent with that position. Once the fish have arrived at the terminal areas, it is difficult for them to argue for more fishing than had originally been agreed to. Yet there are strong incentives to do so, particularly if the rest of the season has been poor.

---

17. *Hoh v. Baldridge,* 522 F.Supp. 683 (1981), now known as *Hoh v. Verity.*

What in many cases appear to be neutral technical issues contain a number of areas over which the two parties often disagree. First, a variety of models can be used to estimate run size, all of which yield somewhat different results. Estimated run size is a prediction about how many fish would have reached the spawning ground absent intercepting fisheries. It involves assumptions about natural mortality, incidental mortality (the number of fish that die as a result of being hooked), and adult equivalents (since many of the fish caught in the ocean are immature). Nor are there universally accepted models of stock composition—the percentage of fish from each of the seven river systems that are present in any mixed-stock area. Making predictions about the impact of intercepting fisheries and drafting the regulations that follow from that turn on such models, and each side has an interest in staking a claim in these areas of scientific uncertainty.

There are a number of fairly subtle allocational implications of using one model rather than another, some of which are well beyond the limited scientific expertise of this author. But one result is quite clear. If the initial run size prediction is high, the fishing regime on the ocean and early season fisheries can be fairly liberal. If that estimate is found to be overly optimistic at the time of the in-season update, fishing effort will have to be scaled back in subsequent fisheries. Since a larger proportion of the ocean catch is taken by nontreaty fishermen, the tribes would then bear a larger share of the conservation burden. On the other hand, if the starting estimate turns out to have been too conservative, fishing in the ocean and mixed-stock areas will have been unduly restrictive, and the fisheries in the terminal and extreme terminal areas (which are mostly tribal) will receive a bonus.

Institutions—Formal and Informal

One consequence of the more-or-less constant litigation between the tribes and the state for the first 10 years after the Boldt decision was that formal rules were established in a great many areas. What is interesting is that for many of the most important issues, formal rules have been superseded by informal institutions worked out between the parties. While the formal rules remain in force and are invoked when all else fails, and the threat to invoke formal rules is frequently used as a bargaining tool during negotiations, it is generally the case that the parties work out their conflicts without resort to formal rules or to the court, through the use of informal rules.[18]

---

18. This is not to say that the court's role was not essential in establishing the parameters within which the two sides must create institutions. In so doing, the court limited the range of potential solutions, and bargaining costs were lowered accordingly.

The Puget Sound Salmon Management Plan.   Judge Boldt's original decision requires that the state work with the tribes on preseason planning and
in-season management. For the first 10 years, coordination and consultation between the two sides was nearly nonexistent, and most controversial
management issues found their way to court, often just moments before a
fishery was scheduled to open. In 1983–84, the two sides jointly negotiated
the Puget Sound Salmon Management Plan (PSSMP), the basic set of
guidelines and schedules under which fisheries are now managed. The
PSSMP requires the parties to agree on preseason run estimates, escapement goals, species management periods (the interval of time during which
fisheries regulations will be directed at that species), and attempts to set
out guidelines for some of the problem areas discussed. Perhaps most
important, it sets time deadlines for when particular management tasks or
agreements between the parties must be completed. The intention was to
introduce some order into the management process and to reduce the
number of decisions that had to be made under the stress of the moment.
Once made, most decisions can only be altered if both parties agree. In
practice, many of the rules and schedules specified in the PSSMP are not
strictly adhered to, although they do provide a floor for negotiations.

Allocation shares.   The basic objective of the Boldt ruling as modified by
the subsequent ruling by the Supreme Court was that treaty and nontreaty
fishermen were each to have the opportunity to catch up to 50 percent of
the harvestable fish destined to pass through the UAPs of the treaty tribes
(*U.S. v. Washington* 384 F.Supp. 312 [1974] and *Washington v. Washington
State Commercial Passenger Fishing Vessel* 443 U.S. 660, 672 [1979]). An
enormous amount of conflict and confusion accompanied the implementation of this rule. The court eventually ruled that the allocational share
was to be balanced, species by species, within each of seven regions. This
division rule currently governs allocation shares. Thus, for the purpose of
allocation, the stocks are lumped together by region of origin, although
for conservation purposes (setting escapement goals), stocks from different rivers but within the same region are treated differently.[19]

Equitable Adjustments and Forgone Opportunities.   In the event that
either side is prevented from catching its share because of a conservation

---

19. Other sources of confusion were whether hatchery fish and natural fish were to be
treated the same for purposes of allocation and whether the catch of nonresidents of Washington state was to be counted as part of the nontreaty share. The court ruled in the affirma-
tive on both questions (*U.S. v. Washington Phase II* 506 F.Supp. 187 [W.D. Wash. 1980]).
There has not yet been a legal determination on the tribes' contention that the catch by
Alaskan fishermen should also be counted as part of the nontreaty share.

closure, they are entitled to an adjustment the following year (in some cases, the payback can extend over a period of time up to five years). If it appears that one side is not going to catch its full share, then the other side may petition to catch both its own share and the remaining share of the other party. If the party that is catching the other party's share can demonstrate that the other side either did not intend or was not capable of catching its share, no subsequent payback is required because it is judged to be a situation of forgone opportunity. This principle was established during the early years when the tribal fleet was fairly small and the state used to claim that it was entitled to fish into the tribal share because the tribal fleet was unable to take its entire allocation. By the early 1980s, the tribes were clearly capable of taking their share and more. Recently this principle has worked against the nontreaty fleet.

Given the zero-sum nature of allocation decisions, it would appear that in any given case, either one side or the other would stand to gain by pressing for an application of the formal rules. In practice, however, that is often *not* the way things are done. For example, the tribes consistently take a larger than 50 percent share of some species in at least two of the seven regions. Projected allocation shares are required as part of the yearly preseason management plan documents, yet they are not included. In addition, end-of-the-year accounting for allocational shares is not done in anything but the most rudimentary fashion. Equitable adjustment claims are rarely filed. The numbers of fish being caught by the two sides simply do not seem to attract the attention that would be anticipated, considering the history of conflict over those very issues.

Three factors account for this apparent discrepancy with what both the rules and the considerations of narrow, short-term rationality would dictate. The most significant of these factors is probably that any particular decision is embedded in a whole series of management decisions on fisheries in other areas or in other management issues. Similarly, decisions today are linked with decisions that will continue to be made by the same parties into the indefinite future. If one party insists on being bound by the rules in one case, the other party is likely to call up another rule on some other occasion. As workers in some labor unions recognize when they employ a "work to rule" strategy for wearing down management opposition during contract negotiations, rigid adherence to the rules is seldom an efficient outcome. That is particularly true here because invoking formal rules may set off a flurry of legal actions and incur costly legal fees. As long as overall accounts are roughly consistent with whatever allocational split the parties have tacitly agreed upon, which from the point of view of the two sides need only be one that makes both parties better off, each side must weigh carefully what it might gain in a particular instance by insisting on an imposition of the formal rules with what it might lose. What we have in effect is a cooperative outcome to situations where mutual rigid rule adherence is an outcome both parties would like to avoid. To bring that about, each party must resist the occasional temptation to employ certain formal rules when doing so would be advantageous.

Consider the following situation, which is enacted annually at the preseason Pacific Fisheries Management Council meetings. Every year there is at least one weak stock that is in danger of falling short of the jointly agreed upon escapement goals. Due to the mixed-stock problem, this stock will be adversely affected by the ocean fishery. On the other hand, meeting the escapement goal would likely entail a complete curtailment of the ocean fisheries and force fishermen to forgo fishing on perhaps 40 to 50 strong, healthy stocks. Under the formal rules, the tribe or tribes that fish in the relevant river system can insist on trying to meet the escapement goal. The state must negotiate successfully with the tribe or tribes in order to meet the needs of an important constituency.[20] The fact that the ocean fishery normally does take place should not obscure the fact that this is an informal agreement, held together by a web of similar agreements on other matters of concern to the tribes.[21]

A second factor highlights the importance of conflicts between different factions of nontreaty fishermen, which at this stage of state-tribal relations sometimes overshadow the issue of relative shares between the treaty and nontreaty fleets. In the South Sound region, for example, four tribes have UAPs in the area and fish commercially there, while the state's primary management objective is recreational fisheries. Since recreational fishers catch relatively few fish, there is a chronic imbalance between the treaty and nontreaty catch. The state could catch its full share only by opening the area on more days to commercial fishermen, but by so doing

---

20. The stakes in such negotiations can be very high. For example, in 1990, the Skagit River wild coho run was weak and became the "driver stock" in preseason negotiations. Had the Skagit River tribes (the Swinomish, Upper Skagit and Sauk-Suiattle) required that the state adhere to the escapement goal, it would have had to catch approximately 86,000 fewer coho salmon, mainly in the ocean. At between $40 and $50 per fish (the standard range used by the state in calculating the value of a fish caught by a recreational fisher), the state's loss would have been somewhere between $3.3 and $4.3 million. (See "1990 Mixed Stock and Terminal Fishery Options Summary for Coho Salmon," reproduced in *U.S. v. Washington,* Civil No. 9213, Klallam and Skokomish Tribes' Memorandum in Support of Suquamish Tribe's Motion for Preliminary Injunction re 1990 Fishery.)

21. Washington Department of Fish and Wildlife officials note that it is a source of some frustration to them that recreational fishermen and charter boat operators often seem unaware of the fact that having a fishing season in the ocean every year is not a foregone conclusion, but rather the product of skillful, delicate negotiations (Turner interview 1993).

they would antagonize the recreational fishers, who are a powerful lobby. A similar situation exists in the North Coastal rivers, where the state could even out allocational shares by allowing nontreaty commercial net fishing but chooses not to because of potential conflicts between sport fishermen and commercial net fishers.

In all other regions fished by both commercial and sport fishermen, the same conflicts make it difficult for the state to use the formal rules in its favor. As discussed earlier, preliminary run size estimates are updated when the fish reach the terminal areas. If the run size has been estimated conservatively and it now appears there are more harvestable fish, the allocational share goes up and the tribes will catch more. The state could take its additional share by opening a nontreaty net fishery, but doing so would be contrary to the expectations of sport fishermen, who tradition-ally are the only nontreaty fishermen in the rivers. As a former director of the Washington State Department of Fish and Wildlife says, "Non-Indian net fisheries in the river are just not part of the culture; we just don't do it" (Turner interview 1993). The tribes have no such cultural prohibition, nor do they have to contend with recreational fishermen. They are therefore ideally positioned to take not only their own share, but also to claim forgone opportunity and harvest the portion of the state's share left unharvested.

Nor is the state in any better position when the in-season update causes the estimated run size to be adjusted downward. Since the non-treaty commercial fleet has already taken its share (calculated on the ear-lier, more optimistic estimates), it will have in effect fished into the treaty share. The tribes can then claim an equitable adjustment, and the state will be forced to pay them back the following year(s). In both of these instances, the unintended consequences of the institutional arrangements the state has worked out in structuring conflicts between factions among nontreaty fishermen are to prevent the state from making the most of for-mal rules.[22]

Another retreat from the formal rules is end-of-the-year accounting, which is currently done in only the most cursory way, for several reasons. First, end-of-the-year accounting for allocational shares is an expensive, time-consuming, and complicated process. Second, the high level of sci-entific uncertainty generates high transaction costs. The same multiplicity of models and assumptions about adult equivalents, natural mortality,

---

22. A former director of Washington Department of Fish and Wildlife notes that non-treaty fishermen perceive the rules as unfair. "The perception in the non-Indian community is that we lose on both sides of that coin. We *do* lose on both sides of that coin, but few peo-ple understand why, that in fact it is a consequence of the state's decision to pursue all this lit-igation and lose it all" (Turner interview 1993).

and incidental mortality that cause problems for in-season allocations are present here, and the uncertainty surrounding such models raises the costs of reaching agreement. Third, neither the Washington Department of Fisheries nor the tribes stands to gain by publishing figures that reflect a disparity between allocational shares, because to do so would invite criticism from either one side or the other.

Dispute Resolution.   In 1975, the court established a dispute resolution forum to hear technical management conflicts between the parties. The Fisheries Advisory Board (FAB) is comprised of a tribal representative, a state representative, and a permanent chair, a fisheries expert who is appointed by the court. It was in part designed to help the court make its way through the labyrinth of technical issues it was to become involved in by retaining jurisdiction over the case. The existence of such a dispute resolution forum became especially important in 1977, when the court assumed day-to-day responsibilities for managing fisheries.

A Fisheries Advisory Board meeting can be called by either side, and it is actually a requirement that all technical disputes go through the FAB process before the court can be asked to consider them. During the proceedings of an FAB, the two sides present their positions and the chair acts as facilitator by attempting to help them reach a solution. If that fails, one side or the other is likely to ask for the chair's recommendation. When the recommendation is made (at which time it is also reported to the court), the parties then have the option of adopting it or continuing the dispute in court. The latter course is rarely taken, however, because it is exceedingly rare for the court to overrule a decision made by the FAB chair.

For the first 10 years after the Boldt decision, FABs were extremely frequent, sometimes 20 per month in the busiest part of the fishing season and totaling more than 100 per year in several years. By the early 1990s there are only one or two in a year. Here we have a very good example of how the tribes and the state have created informal institutions for conflict resolutions that trump formal institutions.

When the formal dispute mechanism is used, several informal rules have evolved to make the process more efficient. The first is that lawyers are not allowed to directly participate in FABs. They may be present and they may even speak quietly into the ear of their client, but it is generally understood that they will not directly participate. No one seems to know the origins of this rule. A second informal rule deals with how costs of the FAB process are shared. FABs are normally held via conference calls, and the rule is that the party that calls the FAB is the party that pays for it. Both of these would seem to be efficiency-enhancing institutions, the first because it discourages posturing and helps limit the parties to discussing the technical, biological issues and the second because it attaches a price to bringing in a third party to adjudicate issues and thus encourages the parties to deal with differences directly.

Complementary Management or Duplication of Effort?

The state and the tribes are engaged in joint production, even if their collaboration has come about as a result of court orders. Ideally, this collaboration would allow each side to concentrate on areas of management where it had a comparative advantage. Tribal fisheries are geographically bounded, and it could be expected that individual tribes have an intimate knowledge of local environmental conditions affecting the stocks in their particular areas. Furthermore, each tribe has clear incentives to protect the particular stocks on which they rely. Conversely, the state may be better equipped to develop comprehensive management plans that incorporate information from far-flung areas. With an evolution toward more efficiency-enhancing institutions, we would expect to see the two sides combining their relative strengths, rather than duplicating each other's efforts.

In certain areas this combining of strengths appears to be happening; in others progress is much slower. In some instances, the parties have been able to develop informal practices that allow them to take advantage of their different capabilities to reduce particular management uncertainties. For example, if a test fishery catches fewer fish than expected, it could mean either that the run is weaker than anticipated (in which case the fishery may need to be closed) or that the run is simply behind schedule because of peculiar environmental conditions and no change in regulations is necessary. If reliable, detailed information about local conditions is readily available, it could result in better management. But since information of this sort is used to make decisions about whether fishermen will be allowed to continue fishing, there are incentives for tribal biologists to act strategically in communicating such information to their counterparts in state offices. However, strategic misinformation on the tribe's side could be matched by defection on the state's side (the state might try to impose a conservation closure or in some other way force the tribes to expend resources in showing why fishing should proceed in each and every circumstance where there was even a small risk). Both the cooperative and the noncooperative outcomes are represented in situations with different tribes.

An example of a clearly productive division of labor between the tribes and the state is the Watershed Planning Process, whereby in a series of meetings, state and tribal fisheries managers and biologists identified both general and particular habitat problems that limited the production of fish. The state bears the largest financial responsibility for restoring habitat, so generally the state does the actual site work and planning. Occasionally the state and the tribes enter into a joint venture; for example, the state might do the original site work and the tribes might carry on the day-to-day maintenance. Another area where the tribes and the state cooperate is with respect to stream spawning surveys, which involve having crews walk along river banks and count the number of spawning salmon *redds* (nests).

Duplication of Effort.   On the other hand, for many types of management activities, there is considerable duplication of effort. For example, both the state and the tribes have devoted substantial resources toward developing the capability to conduct parallel modeling exercises in planning the yearly fisheries. In the very early stages of comanagement, there was a high degree of asymmetry between the tribes and the state with respect to technical information of the sort necessary to predict run sizes. In addition, there was (and is) considerable scientific uncertainty with respect to a number of important issues bearing on questions of run size estimates and stock composition. Since both of these factors create opportunities for strategic misrepresentation, the already high search and bargaining costs involved in jointly managing fisheries were further magnified.

From the early 1980s onward, there was considerable narrowing of the gap between tribal and state-generated predictions of run sizes and similar "technical" questions. As the tribes hired professional staffs, the technical capabilities of the tribes (collectively) now rival and perhaps surpass those of the state, and the tribes now bargain from a position of parity. The combined state and tribal capabilities may represent an overinvestment in research, statistical modeling capacities, and other technical or scientific data collection, where in some cases the parties duplicate each other's efforts. On the other hand, achieving parity between the tribes and the state may have been a necessary phase of development that now makes it possible for the two sides to move away from duplicative research into more collaborative efforts.[23] And it is undeniably the case that an unintended consequence of the initial mutual distrust between the two sides is that there is now an enormous amount known about salmon ecology in this region. It is highly doubtful that it would have happened without comanagement.

---

23. Recently there has been a trend toward more joint research ventures. These include the previously noted study evaluating the methods used to estimate sport catches and an exhaustive inventory of salmon and steelhead stocks completed in 1992.

Administrative Costs. The administrative costs of managing the fishery have risen dramatically since the advent of comanagement, but much of that increase is attributable to the need to address habitat issues in an increasing number of forums and a burgeoning population of recreational fishers. Resource management agencies throughout the country report higher administrative costs due to greater participation by user groups. Still, a significant portion of that increase is attributable to the demands of comanagement. (Pattillo interview 1992).

At first glance, increased administrative costs would seem to indicate considerable inefficiency. Routine harvest management decisions that could be (from a resource management perspective) made by biologists often require consultation with policy analysts (Fraidenburg interview 1992). It is easy to see why that would be the case; once the state recognized the inevitability of joint management, it sought to establish management practices that would minimize conflict with the tribes. Doing so required a major reorientation of the decision rules that comprised the existing bureaucratic culture, a costly and difficult process. To the extent that the comanagers were then able to negotiate difficult issues without recourse to the courts, it may have been an efficient use of resources. A failure to solve bargaining problems is likely to preclude any more efficient division of labor.[24] And there are indications that key decision-makers subsequently began countering this trend by transferring more management authority to lower level staff. Given the usual assumptions about bureaucratic incentives, it seems doubtful, however, that such an initiative would lead to destaffing at the administrative levels.

Conservation. In most situations involving renewable resources, a necessary condition for a set of resource management institutions to be efficient is that the rules ensure sustainable patterns of use. In this case, the formal rule is a standard that is intended to prohibit both overexploitation and waste. This is necessarily a rather elastic criterion, subject to differing interpretations. In general, the state takes a more cautious position on conservation issues than do the tribes, and it is common for tribes to lobby for fishing openings that at least some of the state biologists are not happy with. And there is a popular perception that tribes tend to overfish.

At first glance, this state of affairs appears to support the traditional view, which suggests that given the opportunity, user groups will overex-

---

24. This problem is similar to the shirking problem discussed in chapter 1, with two differences. First, high bargaining costs here produce an overinvestment in some activities; in the earlier case, they produce an underinvestment. Second, and this point is obviously related, is that since both the tribes and the state receive their funding from taxpayers rather than revenue, these activities in effect receive a subsidy.

ploit resources. Much of this discrepancy between the positions of state and tribal managers on conservation issues is illusory, since as discussed in the previous section, both the tribes and the state raise such issues, although they do so at different points in the fishing season. Excess fishing by the tribes appears worse because it occurs at a time when there are fewer fish remaining. Yet overfishing in the marine and other preterminal areas, in which the state is more likely to engage, has the additional danger of being far more indiscriminate with respect to taking immature fish. Given the incentives operating on managers from either system, it is likely that neither, acting alone, can easily arrive at decisions that strike a balance between conservation and utilization. Thus, the current arrangement, which allows either side to challenge the other on conservation grounds, is probably an efficient division of authority.

Comprehensive Fisheries Management.   Perhaps the most striking contribution of comanagement has been to focus attention on the needs of individual stocks. Traditionally, state management has focused on aggregations of species. For both cultural and economic reasons, tribal fisheries management has centered on the stocks that home to their respective regions. This emphasis has forced more attention and stricter regulations aimed at protecting particular stocks, particularly wild stocks.[25] According to one tribal fisheries manager,

> While management may be more decentralized today than prior to the decision in *U.S. v. Washington,* it is far more unified and complete within the State of Washington than it has ever been before. State and federal fisheries managers, because of their concerns for matters of regional importance, have paid painfully little attention to either the needs of the resource in the freshwater environment or the limits within which exploitation of individual stocks must be kept. These are the areas in which state and federal management have historically been most deficient and the areas where the tribal presence is most keenly felt. Tribes filled a glaring void in the prior management scheme: the need to fully consider impacts upon the individual stocks that comprise the resource base. (Morishima 1987, 12)

Monitoring and Enforcement.   Finally, comanagement has been quite successful in reducing transaction costs associated with monitoring and

---

25. The fact that the resource is now being comanaged has resulted in more research being done on wild stocks, which has had the result of bringing to light the severe problems some stocks are experiencing. An unfortunate consequence is that the comanagers themselves may now be receiving more of the blame for stock problems than they deserve.

enforcement. Illegal fishing is estimated to have been significantly reduced since the period prior to the onset of comanagement.[26] State and tribal enforcement personnel are able to work productively together, and a cross-deputation program is in operation in some areas (Mathews interview 1993). As will be demonstrated in a subsequent chapter dealing with tribal management, tribal communities possess a number of resources that they have been able to bring to bear on monitoring and enforcement problems. Delegating management authority to local groups has by all accounts increased the legitimacy of the regulatory regime, which at least arguably is a major factor in the improvement in compliance.

Conclusion

In the 20 years since the Boldt decision mandated comanagement, there were enormous changes in the institutions regulating the salmon fishery and structuring relations between the participants. The first decade was marked by almost continuous conflict in the courtroom and on the fishing grounds. The regulatory system was essentially paralyzed by the combined forces of illegal fishing, ceaseless challenges to regulatory initiatives undertaken by either party, and an almost complete lack of direct communication between the two sides on everything from general policy to specific policy issues. By the late 1970s, the management system had become a textbook example of how little a regulatory body can accomplish when faced with stiff resistance. In other words, it illustrates how costly and ineffective is a system based entirely on formal rules and backed only by formal authority.

This system contrasts sharply with the system operating in the mid-1990s, in which joint planning for the season proceeds in a fairly orderly fashion, in which there are rarely more than a few formal disputes in a year, where the tribes and the state present joint public workshops on cooperative management, and where both sides generally speak positively of one another. While some remaining issues between one or more tribes and the state are currently pending in court, they concern fairly peripheral issues and do not disrupt the overall stability of the system.

This is not to say the system operates flawlessly. Some tribal managers continue to assert that state regulatory agencies are paternalistic and entirely too quick to meddle in tribal management. Some state fisheries department staff members feel that the resolution of genuine problems is being sacrificed in the name of maintaining harmonious relations. Others

---

26. See the chapters on Indian fisheries in Washington State Department of Fisheries Annual Reports 1956–72 for persistent complaints of illegal Indian fishing.

are more sanguine about the current system and more optimistic about its future. One state manager states:

> I believe that the only way we're going to be able to address the long-term conservation of all these stocks that we all care about is through cooperation. And you don't snap your fingers and get cooperation between 20 tribal fishing entities and the Departments of Fisheries and Wildlife. It takes a long time to evolve that kind of trust relationship. Where are we now—almost 20 years since 1974—we've probably got another 10 more years before everyone you talk to feels like it is a good thing. (Scott interview 1993)

Nearly everyone agrees that the current system is a tremendous improvement on the first 10 years. While many wild stocks have declined, this is a large problem throughout the region and not limited to the areas governed by comanagement. Continuing inertia with respect to habitat issues is a long-term threat to the productivity of the systems as a whole, although there may not be a great deal more that either the state managers or the tribes can do about that without a stronger commitment from federal, state, and local government.

CHAPTER 5

Intertribal Conflict and Cooperation

Tribes are separate entities whose interests collide nearly as often as they converge. The ease with which such conflicts can be overlooked testifies to their capacity for acting collectively when negotiating with large, relatively powerful agencies like the Washington State Department of Fish and Wildlife and the Pacific Fishery Management Council or with Canada and Alaska. Tribes also cooperate in maintaining supratribal organizations and contribute to joint fisheries research and enhancement projects. Obviously it is not merely shared economic interests that explain such instances of successful collaboration—members of different tribes also share many common experiences, not the least of which has been their struggle to regain and defend fishing rights. Despite their many common interests, their very real sense of solidarity, and their success in creating and maintaining a variety of institutions that facilitate successful collective action, knotty problems remain, and intertribal litigation has recently far overshadowed litigation between the state and the tribes.

This chapter explores cooperation and conflict between the tribes, examining solved and unsolved collective action problems while attempting to explain what accounts for these different outcomes. Where such problems have been solved, generally through the creation of new institutions, it tries to illuminate the underlying principles structuring their design. Both this chapter and the next deal with areas where groups have considerable autonomy in designing institutional structures. Furthermore, since these institutional structures are of recent origin, the imprints of political struggles are clearly visible. Thus, they shed light on how distributional conflicts and competing values of efficiency and equity are balanced in day-to-day decision making.

In this chapter I first examine the shared and competing interests that lie beneath the surface of intertribal relations. Much of this discussion centers on issues relating to intertribal allocation, which is, not surprisingly, the most intractable of intertribal problems. Next, I discuss a number of potential allocation principles, most of which have been proposed by one tribe or another since the early 1980s. These potential principles are contrasted with the actual institutions that continue to be developed by the tribes in organizing their joint utilization of the resource. The entire set of allocation principles is evaluated in terms of efficiency, equity, and potential for disrupting existing distributional patterns. I then look at supratribal organizations and finally attempt to draw some conclusions from the successes and failures of intertribal cooperation.

Shared and Competing Interests between the Tribes

The Allocation Problem

The underlying logic of the fundamental problem facing the tribes is simple, although situations where these conflicts are played out are often exceedingly complex. Tribes must compete among themselves for portions of what is now a scarce resource. In 1974, the tribal share was less than 5 percent of the total salmon harvest. Once the share was increased to 50 percent, the need for specific intertribal sharing arrangements initially seemed far from urgent.[1] Yet despite the state's concerted efforts to block implementation of the decision, by 1980 the tribes were taking nearly 43 percent of the harvestable salmon (Cohen 1986, 155). The tribes now consistently take the full treaty share, and the problems associated with the allocation of a scarce resource between competing, sovereign tribes have become increasingly salient.[2]

Overcrowding is one of several collective action problems associated with the management of common-pool resources, so it is not surprising that tribal fishermen have had difficulty in this area. What has surprised many observers is the speed with which some tribal fishing fleets expanded. A number of factors contributed to this expansion. Not only was there significant in-migration during the late 1970s and early 1980s as tribal members moved back to the reservation (partly to take advantage of new economic opportunities created by newly affirmed fishing rights), but in the decade following the Boldt decision, the number of tribes covered by it expanded from 14 to 20, as tribes successfully petitioned the federal government for recognition (and treaty fishing rights). In addition, the federal government made low-interest loans available to Indian fishermen seeking

---

1. The historical Indian share was about 2 percent (*U.S. v. Washington,* 1032, 1051). During the late 1960s, the Washington Department of Fisheries adopted policies that allowed the tribes to catch a somewhat larger share.

2. Along with the standard incentives to "stake out a claim" in a common-pool resource, the tribes were given further impetus to expand quickly by the Washington Department of Fisheries periodic threat to try to have the treaty share reduced if the tribes were unable to harvest it completely.

to enter the fishery or upgrade their equipment. The end result has been that overcrowding is now severe enough that most tribal fishermen, like their counterparts in the nontreaty fishery, have great difficulty securing even a moderate income from fishing.[3]

Unlike the nontreaty fishery, where fishermen fish anywhere competition drives them, the tribes' fishing rights are spatially defined. Although one or more treaty tribes have rights to fish in any and all areas throughout Puget Sound and along the Washington coast, by court order, each tribe is limited to specified geographical areas corresponding to the "usual and accustomed places" (UAPs) fished by the individual "tribes" at treaty time.[4]

In general, the UAPs of the treaty tribes radiate out from their reservations (see map 3). Some tribes have far-flung UAPs that extend through several river drainages and encompass both riparian and marine areas (Lummi, Swinomish and others). Others are limited to the terminal area of a single river system (Sauk-Suiattle, Stillaguamish, and Upper Skagit, among others). Most fishing areas are shared by more than one tribe with overlapping UAPs. For example, the North Sound region is shared by the Lummi, Tulalip, Suquamish, Nooksack, and Swinomish; the Skagit River drainage area by the Sauk-Suiattle, the Upper Skagit, and the Swinomish; and the South Sound region by the Puyallup, Muckleshoot, and Nisqually tribes. One area (Department of Fisheries Area 9, which is just north of Seattle) is shared by eight tribes, with a combined fishing capacity that strains the biological health of the runs and the capacity of fish biologists to regulate catch effort.

While *U.S. v. Washington* established *where* each tribe could fish, it did not determine *how much* each tribe was entitled to catch. It is on this question that intertribal conflicts now turn. Without specific allocational institutions, the pattern of interception characteristic of the historical development of the nontreaty fishery is recreated in the treaty fishery, although with the additional complication of spatially defined tribal fishing rights. The institution of UAPs has served to limit overcapitalization, at least among those tribes that fish only in terminal areas where there

---

3. At the same time, some tribal fishermen have profited handsomely.

4. These areas have been defined by the federal court so as to include "every fishing location where members of a tribe customarily fished from time to time at and before treaty times, however distant from the then usual habitat of the tribe, and whether or not other tribes then also fished in the same waters" (*U.S. v. Washington,* 384 F.Supp.312 [W.D. Wash. 1974], 353, 12), which relied on testimony by anthropologists. The inconclusiveness of the anthropological record, plus that fact that "tribes" are a recent and imperfect reconstruction of intergroup relations, has meant that determination of "usual and accustomed places" (UAPs) has been a highly controversial process. Tribes continue to try to expand the scope of their own UAPs or to challenge the scope of others'.

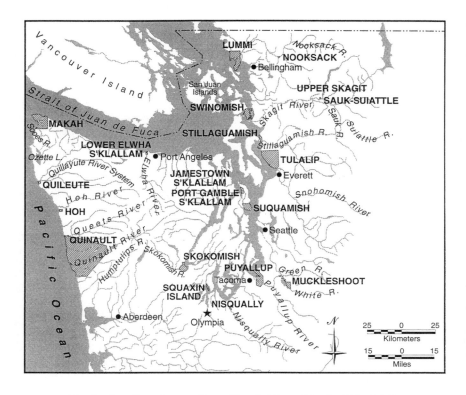

Map 3.   Location of reservations of treaty tribes. (*Map by Blake Feist.*)

is little competitive advantage to having a large, fast, highly efficient boat, but it has created a hierarchy of fishing opportunity in which a tribe's standing depends on where its ancestors fished.[5]

As the fish return to streams of origin, they pass through a succession of fishing areas, each of which has a subset of tribes with recognized fishing rights. Some tribes, by virtue of the location of their UAPs, have access to far more fish than those whose UAPs lie near the end of the migratory path. Tribes with UAPs in marine areas have the opportunity to fish both the stocks that originate in their own areas (terminal areas) and stocks that

---

5. The quality of anthropological evidence that a tribe can muster to support a claim for an expansion of adjudicated UAPs is obviously very important. Since 1974, the court has readjudicated the UAPs of several tribes as a result of proceedings brought by the tribe itself, in trying to expand its fishing areas, or by other tribes, in seeking to restrict that tribe's fishing.

are passing through on their way to other areas. A few tribes, which have large, highly efficient fleets and whose fishing areas include extensive and particularly productive areas (for example, areas where the Puget Sound narrows and the fish are densely concentrated), are more than capable of catching nearly all the treaty share of harvestable fish before they ever reach the South Sound or other terminal areas. South Sound tribes are prevented from competing for "their" fish because they do not have UAPs in preterminal, mixed-stock areas. The effect is that a few favorably situated tribes established themselves early on as major players within the fishery. Other tribes have had to work within this preexisting distributional framework.

Early interception creates management problems for fisheries biologists. As harvest patterns shift to earlier fisheries and fisheries more distant from rivers of origin, management options for protecting weak stocks are limited because fish have not yet separated into discrete stocks. Over time, competition and overcrowding result in harvesting of smaller, immature fish. Both could be expected to be factors in the long-term decrease in the resource.[6]

It is the perception of the South Sound tribes that the resulting distribution is inequitable. South Sound tribes note that although many of their members were among those who fought the hardest to regain their fishing rights, they have received few direct benefits from the fishery. For example, the Nisqually Tribe, many of whose members risked physical violence or jail terms during the "fish-ins" of 1960s and early 1970s, in the period 1987–90 harvested only 2 percent of the treaty share. One year after the Boldt decision, the Nisqually Tribe was harvesting 37,780 fish, approximately 5 percent of the treaty catch. Ten years later, they caught 42,834 fish, but the treaty catch as a whole increased by a factor of more than five and the Nisqually share of the total tribal share decreased to less than 1 percent.

As Nisqually tribal member and longtime fishing rights activist Billy Frank Jr. stated,

> [I] continue reading in the paper of record runs being caught. Where are the record runs being caught? And, yes, they are being caught and people are getting their fishery back. But not the Nisqually people. I read about it in the ocean. I read about it in the Sound. But the Nisqually people are saying "where is our fish?" (Transcript of hear-

---

6. These and other probable effects to unrestricted harvests by tribes at the beginning of the gauntlet were cited by a National Marine Fisheries Service fisheries biologist during legal proceedings brought by several Skagit River tribes against the Makah tribe in 1983 (Civil No. 9213 - Phase I, *Affidavit of Kenneth A. Henry*), August 26, 1986.

ing in *U.S. v. Washington,* Civil No. 9213 - Phase I; Subproceeding 86–5, Sept. 16, 1986)

The allocation conflict pits North Sound tribes against Mid- and South Sound tribes and terminal tribes (those who fish only in the rivers) against those who fish in preterminal (mixed-stock) areas or whose UAPs include both. Often the discussion is cast in terms of tribes that fish in a "traditional" way—in the rivers and with small skiffs or beach seines—opposed to tribes who fish in the mixed-stock, marine areas using modern, highly efficient gear such as large power gillnetters or purse seine boats.[7] Tribes sharing a particular river system or region face crosscutting pressures—they are allies in that they each have an interest in seeing as many fish as possible make it back to their own river systems, yet they face potential conflicts in allocating between themselves once the fish do arrive at or near the terminal areas. In general, conflicts between the tribes were submerged during the periods of strong conflict with the state; they have emerged vividly in the subsequent period.

Common Interests

Both within and outside this arena of competing interests, tribes have a variety of shared interests. For example, although they compete over allocation shares, tribes have a common interest in agreeing, preseason, to a comprehensive yearly fishing plan. Having such a plan allows the tribes to coordinate the ocean, the straits, and Puget Sound fisheries to "share the conservation burden" of protecting weak stocks and to agree on common regulations for fishing areas where tribes share UAPs. Since every tribe has the legal authority to regulate its own fisheries, any tribe can in theory open its fisheries whenever there are harvestable fish remaining in the treaty share. The potential clearly exists for tribes sharing a fishing area (as many as eight in some areas) to be caught up in a competitive race to fish out the available stocks, with all the undesirable side effects that doing so entails. These side effects include overcapitalization, overcrowding, and strong incentives to open treaty fisheries concurrently with nontreaty

---

7. When tribes invoke claims to "traditional" ways of fishing (and by inference, claims about their share in what is, after all, a right stemming from a particular identity), it is hard to know whether they are simply making a virtue out of necessity or expressing a distinct view about what is entailed in making claims to entitlements based on cultural identity. The fact that all the tribes that bring up the issue of "traditional" fisheries are among those restricted to terminal river fisheries and none of the tribes with mixed-stock fisheries raise this issue seems to indicate strategic action. On the other hand, the sincerity of expressions by many tribal members of the value of traditional ways of doing things cannot be disputed.

fisheries, with the resultant congestion and potential for conflict. Even more important, over the long term, such a scenario narrows management options and makes it difficult to regulate fishing in a way that is consistent with sound biological principles.

Without agreement on a preseason intertribal fishing plan, there are apt to be flurries of emergency litigation throughout the season as tribes in both concurrent and successive fisheries work through their differences in the final days and hours before fishing actually begins. Such legal action is costly, in terms of both litigation expenses and the stress it causes among fisheries management staff. It also reduces predictability. And finally, it is in the collective interest of the tribes to resolve internal differences prior to entering into the yearly round of negotiations with the state or Pacific Fishery Management Council (and in some years, with Canada and Alaska during the Pacific Salmon Treaty meetings) lest the state or other participants treat disarray among the tribes as an opportunity to advance their own interests. But agreeing to an annual fishing plan is difficult because it has clear allocational consequences.[8]

A second set of collective interests concerns the creation of incentives to encourage investments in hatcheries and in habitat protection. Here again, the failure to reach agreement on a satisfactory allocation formula causes difficulties because of consequent uncertainties over which tribes will be the beneficiaries of increased productivity. Yet there is more to it than meets the eye. How interceptions affect incentives to invest in hatchery or habitat protection is not entirely straightforward. If the relationship between investments in production and enhancement and the potential returns from that investment were direct, we would expect to see that incentives to invest would be proportionately reduced as the potential of interception increased. This is one "efficiency" argument used by terminal-area tribes—that it is in the best interests of all the tribes that terminal-area tribes be given assurances that their investments will bring benefits to them and that without such assurances, they will have little reason to make such investments. That this is true is not entirely clear, however, since the tribes are able to pass on most of the costs of investment in production and enhancement to the state or federal government. Even if a tribe were to reap *no* benefits from hatcheries in terms of increases in catches, it would still be able to create jobs, at least some of which are likely to be held by tribal members. On many reservations, unemployment rates are 50 percent or more, so job creation is not a trivial matter.

---

8. The fear of becoming a victim of the phenomenon known as "blaming the messenger," especially in the current period of declining fish runs, is probably partly responsible for the reluctance of some tribal representatives to complete preseason negotiations of comprehensive fishing plans.

At the same time, it seems clear that unrestrained interceptions will have some effect in diminishing incentives for investment in hatchery production and habitat preservation. This assumption is logical since at least some potential funding sources give tribes a certain amount of latitude on where the money will be spent. A tribe that expects to see little return on hatchery investment—other than job creation—may put the money to another use.

Similarly, preservation and restoration of fish habitat are areas where tribes want assurances that their efforts will result in larger catches in the future. Here the investment is in lobbying and other expenditures of political capital. There are a number of forums where the tribes can aggressively push state and local government for better habitat protection. Yet tribes must continually weigh the costs and benefits of such expenditures of political capital. As veteran activist and Nisqually tribal fishery manager Billy Frank, Jr. explained to the court in 1986,

> I cannot justify all the time that has been put in there [the Nisqually River drainage] . . . How can you justify talking to George Weyerhaeuser and asking him for buffer zones and how can you ask him to be cooperating in some of the roads and fixing some of the problems up there that we've been involved with? And they've been responsive to some of our concerns and we've been working together on that drainage. How can you justify talking to the farmers on that drainage, to clean up their places along the streams? You know, how can you justify talking to the United States Army? Across the stream the United States Army was going through the creeks, the spawning beds with their tanks. They got cement bridges now. You know, how can you justify that if there's no fish? You can't. (Transcript of Hearing in *U.S. v. Washington,* Civil No. 9213, subproceeding 86–3, Sept. 16, 1986)

The threat of a full-fledged trial to adjudicate each tribe's respective allocation rights has shadowed the tribes for more than a decade. It was narrowly averted in 1986 by a court-ordered mediation that left the parties, if not entirely satisfied, at least resigned. Since then, the resource itself has declined due to habitat deterioration, as well as poorly understood factors involving El Niño conditions, ocean survival rates of coho and chinook, and other natural causes. The case was reactivated in 1994 by the three South Sound tribes and one of the two Mid-Sound tribes. A settlement was reached in 1996.

A lengthy trial and legal resolution of intertribal conflicts is anathema to all tribes except those that are least well-off under present arrangements. They, too, would prefer that a resolution came from the tribes themselves rather than the court. The tribes have a number of reasons to be wary of an all-out legal battle over allocation issues, which they would prioritize as follows: (1) Litigation would be "bloody"—it would cause irreparable harm to intertribal relations. (2) In the course of litigation, one or more tribes might present arguments that could subsequently be used against the tribes collectively by some other party. For example, a tribe might assert that others have exceeded the "moderate income" standard set by the Supreme Court,[9] or tribes might present arguments that would question the right of certain tribes to be federally recognized. (3) Litigation would be expensive. Even if some costs can be passed on to the federal government via the BIA, any court proceeding involves a considerable investment of fisheries staff time and energy. (4) There could be negative publicity created by prolonged, public intertribal wrangling. The tribes work very hard at building a reputation as cooperative, productive groups that undertake a number of projects that have beneficial effects for the larger public. Intertribal conflict and scrambling for economic advantage is inconsistent with that image (and presumably, with their own sense of cultural identity). That partially explains why the tribes work very hard at resolving disputes through some means other than pursuing them in court. Litigation also carries serious psychological costs. Many tribal leaders have close personal ties with one another, many individuals are related through marriage, and in general, tribal members place a high value on maintaining good intertribal relations. The adversarial nature of legal proceedings would result in significant financial and psychological costs for all the participants.

All of the aforementioned points are collective action problems—there is at least one other outcome that would be an improvement upon having no rule at all. Any general principle of allocation would reduce uncertainty, which would limit intertribal conflict, encourage productive investment (in the form of hatcheries or other types of enhancement), and discourage unproductive investment in the form of bigger, faster boats and other forms of overcapitalization. But whatever set of rules or principles is chosen will have readily apparent distributional effects. The bargaining problems that result have in some cases precluded solutions, at least at the level of agreement on fundamental allocational principles.

---

9. In reviewing the *U.S. v. Washington* decision, the Supreme Court upheld Judge Boldt's ruling in all substantive areas. It did modify the treaty-nontreaty sharing formula slightly, so that 50 percent was now the maximum treaty share (the Boldt formula was 50 percent plus ceremonial, subsistence, and on-reservation catch). The Court also noted that "Indian treaty rights . . . secures [*sic*] so much as, but not more than, is necessary to provide the Indians with a livelihood—that is to say, a moderate living" (*Washington v. Washington State Commercial Passenger Fishing Vessel Association et al.*, 443 U.S. 658 [1979], 686–87).

Intertribal Allocation

When these problems began to attract attention in the late 1970s and early 1980s, there were two parallel developments. One signaled the beginning of an ongoing discussion of possible principles that the tribes might use to govern intertribal allocation. This discussion concerns general principles that could be used as the basis for deciding any particular conflict. The tribes have been unable to agree on any of them, for reasons that will be discussed shortly. The second development emerged from the fact that even without agreement at the metalevel of fundamental principles, the tribes have had to solve day-to-day problems of coordination and competition. Out of this series of jerry-rigged settlements of particular conflicts grew a patchwork of formal and informal agreements. Incrementally, a set of institutions was constructed that the tribes currently use as the framework for annual fishing agreements. The resulting edifice can hardly be said to be divorced from economic self-interest but also reflects nonrational considerations.

In the ongoing discussions between the tribes over which, if any, fundamental principles should govern intertribal allocation, different tribes have argued for radically different criterion. Such claims are a complicated blend of self-interest and competing conceptions of the nature of equity, a not uncommon state of affairs. In this situation as in others, any definition of equity is liable to be contested whenever its distributional consequences become apparent.

Equity

Conceptions of equity generally involve some notion of equality. Yet equality can mean quite different things, depending on what it is applied to and at which point in a process of production and distribution it is being applied. For example, it is entirely consistent with some definitions of equity that there be large inequalities of wealth, provided that these inequalities have resulted from situations in which there has been uniformity of treatment (or equality of opportunity) and that subsequent changes in status are the result of uncoerced exchanges as opposed to theft, deceit, or the like.[10] Obviously, the need to determine an initial starting point and categories of permitted and prohibited subsequent interactions still leaves considerable scope for disagreement. Other accounts of equity

---

10. Many conservatives subscribe to this view. Robert Nozick presents the most cogently argued, exhaustive treatment of this perspective (1974).

treat define it as a property of outcomes or end-states and require any deviations from equality in distribution to be persuasively justified.[11]

One useful way of framing different conceptions of equity is presented by Deborah A. Stone (1988).[12] Stone argues that various standards of equity involve three important dimensions: the relevant characteristics of recipients or recipient groups, the nature of the item that is being distributed, and the social process of distribution. Many of the issues that have emerged in intertribal discussions can be classified under this rubric. The first category groups together questions about who is entitled to share in the tribal allocation. Are tribes or individual tribal members the relevant units of analysis? If the answer is tribes, does any group comprised of descendants of the aboriginal people of western Washington qualify, or only those who belong to groups that have previously satisfied the requirements for federal recognition? If the answer is tribal members, who and what determines who qualifies as a tribal member? Are nonmember spouses entitled to fish? And since all tribes are affected by how each tribe draws its membership boundaries, should these issues be resolved by a mutually agreed-upon common standard?[13]

The second category covers issues related to the nature of the fishing right. Is fishing simply the economic act of producing a commodity, or is it a form of cultural self-expression? If it is the former, then there is no reason to distinguish between individuals (or tribes) on the basis of the use to which they put the exercise of fishing rights, or at least not on these grounds, but if it is at least partly the latter, then equal treatment involves setting up a hierarchy of use rights. Tribes would have to balance seeming incommensurables such as the need to make a living with the need to affirm one's cultural identity and group solidarity.

The third category calls for equal access with respect to the process of allocating rights to fish. According to this concept of equity, challenges to current distributional patterns must demonstrate that there has been something about the series of events leading up to the current allocational pattern that would make it inequitable. A skewed outcome is not in itself reason for reallocation, so long as it has come about through justifiable

---

11. Rawls (1971) is a very persuasive account of the idea that fairness implies a rough equality of outcomes, in which departures from equality need to be justified as necessary for the greater good.

12. Stone credits her approach largely to Douglas Rae and coauthors (see Rae 1979 and Rae et al. 1981).

13. Several tribes have argued that *all* of these issues be put on the bargaining table along with more narrowly construed allocation questions. See Synopsis of Tribes' Legal Responses to Mediator's Final Report in Subproceeding 86–5, Jan. 18, 1990.

actions.Using this approach, some tribes (particularly those who were latecomers to the federal recognition process) argue that through no fault of their own they were for many years effectively shut out of the fishery and that equality of treatment demands that they be given additional opportunities now or at least that their fisheries not be "capped" before they have fully developed. Similarly, several tribes argue that their greater catches result from the fact that they are better fishermen.

A variety of criteria could be defended on one or another conception of equity. In practice, the tribes making the strongest equity arguments tend to make their case in terms of the unacceptability of significantly unequal outcomes. Thus, equity arguments emerge as part of a case to justify principles that would redistribute fishing opportunities and reduce present inequalities.

Efficiency

Perhaps because of its distinctly "underwhelming appeal" (Ellickson 1991), the efficiency-enhancing attributes of a particular principle rarely are what animates discussion of intertribal sharing agreements. But different allocational principles do have such implications, and tribes are not unaware of them. Any allocational principle that reduces uncertainty and increases predictability would be a move in the direction of allocative efficiency, that is, it could potentially increase aggregate utility. It would also reduce litigation and other conflict-related transaction costs. Beyond that, it is generally true (or at least consistent with the arguments made in chapter 2) that allocation principles that reward skill, effort, and productive investment are more likely to result in allocative efficiency than those based on need or some other characteristic unrelated to productive capacity.

Efficiency appears to be a more straightforward concept than equity, but determining whether a particular principle is efficiency enhancing is difficult in practice. For example, policies that encourage productive investment could be expected to enhance allocative efficiency; policies that encourage overcapitalization do not. Yet it is often difficult to determine at what point productive investment becomes overcapitalization or to design principles that discriminate between the two.[14] In addition, the relative efficiency of some principles depends on whether the principle is applied at one particular time (after which outcomes are allowed to develop without interference) or whether adjustments are ongoing. If the participants'

---

14. These practical problems are in addition to those that emerge once we examine more closely what it is that is being maximized. Is it simply net profit from sales of fish, or is there something more to the enterprise of fishing? These issues will be taken up in the final chapter.

expectations are that the second scenario will be followed, they will have incentives to alter their behavior with respect to the attributes relevant to the principle. Attempting to limit such behavior by treating (for example, by public announcement) the initial allocation as a onetime event will not entirely alleviate the problem. Once a particular principle has taken on some measure of legitimacy and stature as the result of the initial distribution, it will be very difficult to argue against subsequent reallocations following the same principle in the event that the distributional patterns that develop at some point in the future are determined to be unsatisfactory on one or more grounds.

Potential Allocation Principles

Since the early 1980s, a number of simple allocation principles have been discussed by the tribes. Any one of these principles would appear to promise an increase in predictability and simplicity as well as fairness (of one kind or another) to the current procedures. In this subsection I describe these principles and consider why none of them has in fact been adopted. Principles 1 through 7 have been proposed by one or more tribes. A couple more principles that are conspicuous by their absence from intertribal discussions—principles that have been widely discussed in comparable, nontreaty settings—are also included here. The high level of sophistication of tribal discussions about this issue suggests that their omission is not due to ignorance, but rather to widely shared beliefs that such principles would be undesirable for one or more reasons. Thus they too have something to add to an understanding of how the tribes approach this issue.

A. Principles Considered by the Tribes
   1. *Shares proportionate to a tribe's size.* This is a strongly redistributive principle that is, not surprisingly, proposed and supported by some of the larger tribes. Unless it were implemented as a one-time-only allocation, it would encourage growth in tribal membership. It does not reward skill, effort, or conservation.
   2. *Shares proportionate to the number of fishermen per tribe.* This is a slightly less redistributive principle, since at any particular point, there will always be more fishermen among the intercepting tribes than among the nonintercepting tribes unless interceptions are limited by some additional rule. Like principle 1, it would encourage new entrants. It also would encounter difficulties with questions of definition. Is a fisherman someone who fishes consistently, or does it include those who throw their net in the water once a season?

3. *Shares based on each fisherman's investment.* This criteria could be defended under some criteria of equity, although objections could be raised on the issue of process—to what extent are current investments a reflection of previous (perhaps inequitable) allocations? And while it avoids the definitional problems of principle 2, it clearly encourages overcapitalization and thus undermines efficiency.

4. *One tribe/one share within each region where a tribe has UAP rights.* This criterion discourages overcapitalization and overcrowding because shares would not be sensitive to increases in the size of the tribe or the size of the fishing fleet. On the other hand, it violates at least some conceptions of equity, and it would require considerable disruption to current distribution patterns. Not surprisingly, small tribes favor this principle.

5. *Shares based on investment in hatcheries and habitat protection.* Tying allocational shares to investments in habitat protection and hatchery facilities is an efficiency-enhancing principle because it enlarges the resource base, but only up to the point where investment ceases to be productive. Investments made subsequent to that point are a form of overcapitalization. Unfortunately, this principle encourages investment in both circumstances, and discriminating between them would likely be difficult.[15] Establishing this principle as the primary grounds for intertribal allocation would doubtless be challenged on equity grounds by tribes with few potentially productive habitat sites or little access to capital.

6. *Shares proportionate to efforts by each tribe in lobbying regulatory agencies, and in pursing litigation to increase the total treaty share.* Partly in response to the discussions of hatchery investments, some tribes have argued that other forms of investment should receive equal consideration. If the relevant group is defined as all treaty tribes, this principle would have efficiency implications similar to enhancement investment.[16] Once again,

---

15. Of course, giving tribes additional shares of fish stocks is not the only means of encouraging hatchery investment. If fish are worth more when caught as they enter the Straits of Juan de Fuca than when they reach the terminal areas (as they are), then a more efficient arrangement might be for terminal tribes to raise the fish, other tribes to catch them, and the two sets of tribes to work out a profit-sharing arrangement. No tribe has suggested such an approach, perhaps in part because of the high transaction costs that would ensue.

16. It is not apparent that such a rule would be efficiency enhancing if the definition of the "group" is broadened to include a larger collectivity, but it is true for solutions to many collective action problems. For example, a group of firms that overcome their collective action problems and obtain an industry-wide subsidy from government may be enriching themselves at the expense of the public.

tribes with little access to capital that could not afford to undertake litigation or to press tribal claims in other forums would be disadvantaged by this principle.

7. *Shares proportionate to the relative quantities of fish taken at treaty time.* Some tribes have suggested that an appropriate allocation principle is one that seeks to replicate the distributional pattern that existed among the tribes at treaty time. The implications for efficiency under such a principle are not entirely clear. If we believe that competition between tribes would have ensured that those who were more efficient would tend to be those who ended up in particularly productive areas, we might conclude that there was an efficiency component to this rule at treaty time. Yet that would not take into account the role of superior coercive capacities, which could also explain the spatial distribution of tribes with respect to particularly productive areas, but had only a limited relationship to efficiency. In any case, since modern technology has drastically altered the way fishing is done, there is little correlation between what was (perhaps) an efficient set of tenure arrangements then and what might be now. In addition, the only way a principle like this could be implemented would be to sharply limit ocean and other mixed-stock fisheries and limit fisheries to terminal areas. This idea has been suggested by a least one economist as a way of minimizing "commons" problems and enhancing efficiency (see Barsh 1991). To do so, however, would involve enormous dislocations of the treaty and nontreaty fisheries that have been established since modern methods and technologies began to be used.

B. Other Principles

8. *Individual Transferable Quotas.* Under this method, divisible quotas (based on predicted run sizes) would be established, distributed according to a previously agreed-upon criterion, and thereafter exchanged through a market. According to most economists, this is the most efficient method of allocation since once a market in quotas has developed, permits are expected to gravitate to the most efficient users. Obviously this line of reasoning presupposes agreement on an appropriate principle for the initial distribution. Tribes are aware of this method, but no tribe has endorsed it and several have specifically rejected it.

9. *Open Competition.* Tribes are currently limited to fishing within their respective UAPs, but there is nothing to prevent them from issuing mutual invitations to each other and thereby allowing open competition between all tribal fishermen throughout the

case area (the same rule that governs the nontribal fishery). Doing so would, of course, encourage overcapitalization and the whole complex of "commons problems" discussed earlier. With the exception of the four coastal tribes, which face a somewhat different fishing environment and who have recently established reciprocal invitational fishing among themselves, no tribes have suggested it.

Efficiency Revisited

We can ask which of these principles of allocation is (allocatively) *efficient* relative to the status quo, that is, which of them would result in a larger total output from a given set of inputs. But determining these relatively efficient principles, though it might satisfy some economists, is not of much practical help, for no rational party would consent to move to one of them unless it would be made better off by the move or at least not made worse off. In other words, the principles of interest are those that are Pareto superior to the status quo (i.e., are preferred to the status quo by some and not less preferred by any), not those that are Pareto optimal (i.e., from which no Pareto superior moves can be made).[17] This idea is not always fully recognized or absorbed by economists and political economists. It is another way of saying what was said earlier: efficiency gains will not be realized by rational agents unless the distributive problem is solved, that is, unless all parties consent to the actual shares that will be theirs under the new state of affairs, and presumably they will not so consent unless they will be at least as well off as they are presently.

The question, then, is which of the nine principles described above is Pareto superior to the status quo and which would therefore be a move to which the tribes, if their concern was to maximize their profits, would consent? The answer is that none of them is. A move to any one of these principles would make at least one tribe worse off, or there would be a least one tribe that would expect that under the operation of the principle, it would sooner or later (probably) become worse off. In some cases, the move would bring about an immediate redistribution of shares among the tribes; in other cases, the move would result in actions (e.g., an increase in investment in gear) by some or all of the tribes, which would result in lower profits for some tribes.

The tribes have even resisted agreeing to freeze the current distribu-

---

17. A move that produces greater efficiency is a "Kaldor-Hicks efficient" move because the gain in output *could* be redistributed so that there were no losers in the move. Such a move could be called *potentially* Pareto superior. But, again, unless it actually *is* Pareto superior, it would not command the assent of all parties. For a full discussion of these concepts of efficiency, see Coleman 1988.

tion of catch. They have in particular considered a proposal to make future shares equal to the average of the last five years' catch. Since each tribe might expect to receive under this rule what it now actually gets (which is the result of the operation of institutions I will describe subsequently), and since using the rule would appear to have the added benefit for all of increased predictability and lessened conflict, one might have expected this rule to be adopted. It has in fact been supported by more tribal representatives than any of the other principles discussed, but some have feared that it would lock them into an allocation upon which they might be able to improve at some time in the future.

Intertribal Institutions

The tribes' inability to agree on any of the simple allocational principles does not mean they lack institutions with which to structure the joint utilization of this resource or to manage the problems that it engenders. There are an array of intertribal institutions, which range across a wide spectrum of formality and specificity. Some have been entered as court orders after being signed by the parties; others exist only as written minutes or oral agreements. Some are made annually, such as the intertribal fishing plans; others remain in force indefinitely. There are informal agreements that are nonetheless adhered to year after year and formal agreements that are invariably contested. There are agreements involving all the tribes, regional agreements among tribes that share a watershed or fish a particular stock (the Sockeye tribes, for example), and subregional agreements between two or more tribes. Intertribal agreements have nearly all been generated *internally;* the court's role has been limited to prodding the tribes to reach agreements and then formalizing and enforcing the agreements at which tribes have arrived.[18]

These institutions, which produce the allocation each year (what I have called the status quo), are complex, not at all like the simple principles considered earlier, and they reflect a concern on the part of the tribes not only for maximizing their profits from fishing, but also for fairness, tradition, and cultural expression. Efficiency gains, even ones achieved by Pareto superior moves, are not the Indians' only concern.

Property Rights

Two broad categories of what could be described as middle-range institutions have been created by the tribes. The first category has been a move-

---

18. The court also set up many of the ground rules, such as the determination of tribal UAPs.

ment toward stricter definition of property rights. The tribes now recognize several different classes of rights in addition to those contained in court-determined UAPs.

Primary fishing rights are the most restrictive class of rights. They exist in areas where tribes share a UAP but where one tribe has been recognized by other tribes to have a particular claim over a subsection within the larger area, for example, a bay that adjoins the reservation. The tribe is then said to have primary or exclusive rights over the area, and other tribes are excluded from fishing in that area unless invited by the tribe whose "home waters" these are. Although it is by no means unheard of for tribes to contest each other's claims to primary rights, the concept of primary rights is universally accepted.

A second category is regulatory or secondary rights, which convey management authority to set regulations. They cover a larger area than primary rights, but they do not include the right to exclude other tribes with UAPs for fishing. A third category is in-common rights, which are areas where all tribes with UAPs are entitled to fish and where each tribe may set its own fishing regulations. One of the strongest conventions, and one that emerged very early, is that tribes that share in-common fishing areas must agree to common fishing regulations. Tribes spend considerable time each year negotiating a preseason comprehensive fishing plan.

The effect of these innovations in property rights is to reduce conflict and increase predictability. And at least in the areas where primary rights have been designated, tribes that wish to can limit overcapitalization through limiting entry. For example, one four-tribe cooperative bans large, highly capitalized purse seine boats in its shared management areas.[19] Many tribes limit participation by large boats in inshore primary waters as a way of ensuring fishing opportunity to small-boat fishermen.

For the Puget Sound tribes, the trend has been to move toward more sharply delineated property rights. For the ocean tribes, the trend has been reversed. Although the Quinaults, the Hoh, and the Quileute designate reservation rivers as the exclusive fishing areas of the respective tribes, they have increased the area available for each tribe's ocean troll fishermen by issuing reciprocal annual invitations to each other's fishing areas. Since fish are more dispersed in the ocean than in Puget Sound, doing so probably facilitates a more cost-effective strategy for fishing.

---

19. Most tribes do not formally limit entry (other than requiring tribal membership, requiring participants to be a certain age, and in some cases requiring residence on the reservation). While this lack of entry limitation is largely due to a perception on the part of tribal leaders that such limitation would be politically unpopular, it is nonetheless the case that without a credible agreement that secures a tribe's share, it would not be rational for it to restrict fishing by its own members.

Allocation Share Agreements

The second type of institution is allocation share agreements. Throughout the late 1970s and early 1980s, a network of agreements governing intertribal sharing grew out of particular conflicts involving particular tribes. By the mid-1980s, the resulting mosaic had become increasingly difficult to coordinate, and intertribal disagreements had begun to spill over into the state-tribal dispute resolution forum. Agreements between particular tribes were continually being compromised by the absence of agreements with other tribes or concerning other stocks. Finally, as a direct result of a lawsuit filed in 1986 by several of the South Sound tribes against the North Sound tribes, a two-year mediation effort attempted to bring all tribes and all species of fish under a comprehensive, long-term plan. Although the Salmon and Steelhead Management Plan (SSMAP) has never been formally ratified by the tribes or entered as a court order, approximately 80 percent of it is adhered to and it forms the departure point for yearly intertribal negotiations (Rutter interview 1993).[20] Rather than attempting to negotiate bedrock principles, the SSMAP codified, coordinated, and rationalized preexisting agreements.[21] The result has been a document that reflects a preoccupation with both efficiency *and* fairness.

Most intertribal agreements contain variations of the following three-tiered sharing formula, in which different sharing formulas are triggered by different levels of abundance.[22]

> *Level 1.* At the level of lowest abundance, the largest share goes to the terminal-area tribes and a relatively small share goes to intercepting tribes. For example, 85 per cent of South Sound–origin fish go to the South Sound tribes, while 15 per cent can be taken by intercepting (North Sound or Mid-Sound) tribes. The principle underlying this tier of the sharing agreement is that in times of relative scarcity, the shares of intercepting tribes should be limited until the terminal tribes are given the opportunity to fulfill the basic needs of their fishermen. The rule, in other words, is motivated by a concern for fairness rather than efficiency.
>
> *Level 2.* At the next level of abundance, the additional fish (in addi-

20. The settlement agreement reached by the tribes in 1996 retains the fundamental outlines of the earlier allocation-sharing agreement.

21. The fact that it did not grapple with fundamental principles or attempt to substantially change existing allocations between tribes was and continues to be a source of disappointment to several of the South Sound tribes (Hage interview 1993; Troutt interview 1993).

22. A similar allocation rule governs some locally managed irrigation systems (Ostrom 1990).

tion to the amount allocated under the first formula) are shared equally between the intercepting tribes and the terminal fisheries. This tier recognizes the political reality that intercepting tribes are capable of taking far more than that and there is not a great deal the South Sound tribes can do about it.

Level 3. At the level of highest abundance, the formula for the additional fish (the difference between level 2 and level 3) is again biased in favor of the terminal tribes. The intention is to reward the terminal tribes for increased hatchery production (and to provide incentives for further productive investments). This rule reflects a concern with allocative efficiency.

Other Allocation Share Agreements

There are some agreements that are not transparently explicable in terms of even enlightened self-interest. A striking example is the late run of Nisqually River chum, which all the tribes have agreed should go entirely to the Nisqually Tribe. The other tribes have even been willing to trade off some of their own share to this run to the state in order that the Nisquallies be allowed to harvest the whole Nisqually River late chum run. Most observers explain this action in terms of the high regard all the tribal representatives have for Nisqually leader Billy Frank Jr., who helped found and is the current director of the tribal umbrella group, the Northwest Indian Fisheries Commission, and whose family was pivotal in the fight to regain fishing rights.[23] Mr. Frank has been a strong advocate for and facilitator of intertribal unity, which has earned him the respect and gratitude of many tribal leaders. In the late 1980s, however, he was coming under increasing criticism from members of his own tribe for not pressing the claims of Nisqually fishermen more strongly. The decision of representatives from other tribes to restrict their own fisheries should be seen as an attempt to ease this pressure.

Intertribal Organizations

After the Boldt decision, the tribes realized that they would continue to have a variety of shared interests that could best be served through the cre-

---

23. Billy Frank Sr., who died at age 104 in 1984, testified in *U.S. v. Washington* and was himself a participant in the "fish-ins" and other similar confrontations, many of which took place at Frank's Landing, a site along the Nisqually River where the Franks have lived for generations. Billy Frank Jr. is the current director of the NWIFC and a very visible representative of the tribes in scores of formal and informal forums. In 1992, he received the Albert Schweitzer Award for Humanitarianism.

ation of an intertribal organization. Such an organization would allow them to take advantage of economies of scale in areas such as the generation of scientific or statistical information, technical and computer training, as well as public relations. In addition, it facilitated the tribes' efforts to bargain as a unified, collective body. The Northwest Indian Fisheries Commission was established in 1974 to "coordinate an orderly and biologically sound treaty Indian fishery in the Pacific Northwest and provide member tribes with a single, unified voice on fisheries management and conservation matters," (NWIFC 1990, 1). The NWIFC's activities are overseen by eight tribal commissioners, who represent the eight watersheds in the area.

Initially the NWIFC helped fill a vacuum in managerial expertise. Although a few tribes had functioning fisheries management departments in place at the time of the Boldt decision, many tribes did not. The NWIFC continues to provide special skills training for tribal managers, especially in computers. It also does a considerable amount of coordination between different tribes in the areas of data collection, hatchery production, and habitat protection and rehabilitation, which provides the tribes with a source of information for comprehensive, systemwide planning. Certain types of costly technology such as code-wire tagging equipment used in stock composition research is owned by the NWIFC and shared by various tribal hatcheries.

The formation of NWIFC was also driven by the need to address problems of asymmetric information existing between the tribes and the state. As the discussion in chapter 4 indicated, the outcome of bargaining over shares often turns on data collection and the ability to justify predictions and escapement goals based on competing scientific models. Although the state was supposed to provide information about run sizes, escapement levels, stock composition, and the like to the tribes, such information was often not forthcoming. Even when it was made available, the tribes often considered it unreliable. One of the most important functions of the NWIFC in the early years was to enable the tribes to do their own run-size predictions and updates, with which it could challenge state-initiated conservation closures of tribal fisheries. The NWIFC continues to provide technical assistance and coordination in annual and long-range fishery management planning. It is particularly active in providing statistical and other technical information to tribal representatives during yearly planning meetings with Canada and Alaska, the Pacific Fishery Management Council meetings, and the species management plans jointly authored with the State of Washington. Members of the commission also do stock composition research, code wire tagging, and generate various other systemwide technical and scientific information.

Currently, NWIFC has a staff of 50 to 55 people. It is funded by the Bureau of Indian Affairs, the Administration for Native Americans, and the U.S. Fish and Wildlife Service. Staff include a quantitative services division, regional planning coordinators, regional biologists, environmental coordinators, and a hatchery and enhancement division. NWIFC objectives and policy are set by eight commissioners, who represent the eight drainage areas in the case area. In one case, a commissioner represents only one tribe (Makah), but in most instances, two or more tribes along a particular river system are represented by each commissioner. Since fault lines between the tribes tend to emerge along spatial lines, this is a good mechanism for ensuring that a balance of interests are represented by the commissioners.

In addition to providing the collective goods discussed earlier, NWIFC performs other tasks associated with political entrepreneurship. An important function of political entrepreneurs is to provide information and facilitate coordination and communication between members of a group.[24] The NWIFC coordinates the activities of different tribes performing similar sorts of activities having interactive effects, such as in the case of hatchery production or habitat enhancement. It encourages tribes to arrive at a unified bargaining position prior to entering into negotiations with external regulatory bodies. And since the mid-1980s, it has increasingly played a role in resolving conflicts over intertribal allocation issues and facilitating formal and informal agreements between tribes.

The fact that the tribes have been quite adept at overcoming the collective action problems involved in providing themselves with organizational structures and at obtaining funding for those services is entirely explicable within standard rational choice theory. The number of tribes is fairly small, and at least initially they were a very homogeneous group in terms of shared interests, beliefs, and a common history that is distinct from majority history and culture. After years of fighting with the state in court and on the fishing grounds, the tribes had a cadre of experienced, talented political leaders who were accustomed to working together and could direct the formation and day-to-day functioning of a professionally trained, largely non-Indian staff of biologists and statisticians. Furthermore, the ratio of costs to benefits was extremely favorable because most of the costs of creating and maintaining the NWIFC could be passed on to other parties. By contrast, resolving conflicts over intertribal allocation has proved to be much more difficult because intertribal allocation is largely a zero-sum game—what one tribe gets is unavailable to another.

---

24. See Frolich and Oppenheimer 1978, chap. 4, and Popkin 1979, 259–66 for discussions of the pivotal role of political entrepreneurs.

There is no apparent way to enlarge the collective share without reordering the shares of individual tribes. While all tribes share an interest in avoiding intertribal conflict, particularly public conflict such as intertribal litigation, a number of tribes stand to lose considerably with any alteration to the status quo.

Conclusion

The tribes are clearly able to overcome barriers to collective action when the benefits of successful collective action are high relative to contribution costs and where they do not encounter high bargaining costs. For example, their success in forming and maintaining the Northwest Indian Fisheries Commission is partly explicable by the fact that it has been funded by the Bureau of Indian Affairs and there is little need to resolve distributional issues regarding cost sharing. Tribes continue to struggle over intertribal allocation issues, and the current organizing principles for their joint utilization of the resource system are not as efficiency enhancing as they could be, largely because disagreements over distributional questions preclude alternative arrangements.

Nonetheless, the tribes go some ways toward solving these problems, much farther, in fact, than do their counterparts in the nontreaty fishery. Every year, the tribes manage to come up with a workable plan for coordinating their joint utilization of an enormously complicated resource. Such a plan involves juggling the needs of 20 tribes, each of which has several disparate groups of fishermen. Although considerable wrangling accompanies this process, their negotiation and decision-making institutions are sufficiently robust so as to allow them to coordinate their fisheries and present a united front to external regulatory agencies.

Overcapitalization is a huge problem in the nontreaty fishery; it is a much smaller problem in the treaty fisheries. Partly through the court's designation of spatially limited fishing rights, but largely through self-generated property rights and allocational share agreements, the tribes have reduced much of the uncertainty that fuels overcapitalization. In situations of open access, the rule of capture determines what individual fishermen can harvest, and they are led to invest in larger and faster boats. This has typically been the situation in the state-managed fishery. Beginning in the mid-1980s, the tribal fishery also had begun to move in that direction. While there are tribes that continue to have significant overinvestments in boats and gear, the overall trend toward overcapitalization was largely brought under control through these intertribal agreements.

To go farther in the direction of solving these and other problems associated with intertribal allocation would require the creation of new institutions (or the recreation of old institutions) that would resolve the distributional problems. Instituting a set of arrangements that have the potential of greater efficiency would produce winners and losers. Unless they receive greater assurances that surpluses will be redistributed, tribes that stand to lose by alterations to the status quo are unlikely to agree to changes. In the precontact era, there were a number of institutions that increased the chances that everyone would be made better off by an increase in the income of one set of actors. Lacking such institutions, the tribes may be forced to look to the court for a further resolution of the intertribal allocation problem and the inefficiencies that accompany it.

Intertribal institutions are the product of resolutions to particular conflicts. They are a reflection of a complex blend of goals and values. While it is incontestable that narrowly rational behavior explains a great deal about the shape of these institutions, it cannot tell the whole story. Considerations of fairness also play a significant role in the structure of intertribal institutions.

CHAPTER 6

Internal Governance

What is remembered about the *U.S. v. Washington* decision is that it gave tribes the opportunity to catch 50 percent of the harvestable salmon. Of equal significance is that the decision restored to tribes the authority to manage their own fisheries. By strictly limiting intervention in a tribe's exercise of its fishing rights, the court reversed a century of state regulation that had forced tribal fisheries to bear the burden of non-Indian overfishing and nearly outlawed tribal fishing in the name of conservation. While granting the tribes close to absolute authority with respect to the regulation of their fishermen, the court did require that the tribes demonstrate technical skills and regulatory capacities necessary to successfully manage the resource.[1]

Thus, the decision in *U.S. v. Washington* was not only a tremendous economic opportunity, but also an enormous political challenge. It ushered in an era of significant institutional innovation as tribes sought to design management structures that would combine professional expertise and regulatory efficacy with participation and accountability. For tribal leaders, it required further refinement of political capabilities. Previous victories had been won through great skill in the arts of strategic confrontation and political communication and the ability to effectively invoke resistance to an external enemy. The nature of the administrative and regulatory tasks that followed was quite different and potentially far more divisive.[2] For example, compiling membership rolls involved defining what constitutes tribal identity in situations where marriage between Indians of different tribes and Indians and non-Indians has been and continues to be common. Deciding who could fish, how the benefits of the fishery were to be shared, and how the tribe would enforce its regulatory authority were all difficult questions.

---

1. As prerequisites to managing their fisheries, the court required the tribes to have well-organized tribal governments, qualified fisheries biologists, managers, and enforcement personnel, an officially approved membership roll, and a means of identifying tribal fishers (*U.S. v. Washington,* 384 F. Supp 312 [1974] 340, 341).

2. The challenge of transforming an insurgency movement into an administrative body capable of governing is discussed by Theda Skocpol (1979).

The tribes had to confront fundamental issues about inclusion and exclusion and balance the demands of professional management with those of democratic accountability while simultaneously battling recalcitrant state agencies. They also had to construct legal and regulatory structures without creating the perception that they were replicating the oppressive authority structures that had characterized state regulation. The fishing decision, then, was a catalyst for institutional growth and development. Just as relations between the tribes and the state were to be significantly altered by participation in cooperative management, the institutional structures of governance within tribes have also been profoundly changed.

How tribes have proceeded in developing their regulatory capacities should tell us something about the ways a local group meets the transaction costs associated with management of a common-pool resource. It should also help illuminate the question of what social values appear to be reflected in institutions that evolve in close-knit, relatively autonomous communities. While close-knit and fairly homogeneous in many respects, the fishermen in most tribal communities are fairly heterogeneous with respect to the type of fishing they do and their relative incomes derived from fishing. The spatiotemporal dimensions of salmon fishing mean that regulatory decisions almost invariably have distributional consequences of which all participants are keenly aware. The close proximity of the regulators to those they are regulating brings a directness and immediacy to decisions about allocation, harvest management, and conservation issues that is not found in the state-managed fishery.[3]

In this chapter, I first introduce the formal regulatory institutions and examine how local managers meet the demands of managing a complex common-pool resource. I then attempt to answer the question of why tribes generally fail to limit entry. What we will find is that tribal communities are able to use their particular strengths and collective capacities very effectively in reducing many of the transaction costs associated with managing a common-pool resource. But instead of it resulting in institutions that enhance allocative efficiency, the institutions in place reflect beliefs about fairness and the value of tradition and tribal identity. At the risk of oversimplifying the situation, it is apparent that fishing is nearly as important as an affirmation of a distinct identity as it is an economic activity.

---

3. One Washington State Department of Fisheries biologist points out that it would be extraordinary for a group of nontreaty fishermen to arrive in the office of a state fisheries manager to complain about a fishing closure. The biologist suggests that it would not be uncommon in a tribal fisheries office, however, and that in turn puts a great deal of pressure on tribal fisheries managers to open fisheries that are unwise from a biological perspective (Interview A 1992).

Transaction Costs in the Context of Local Communities

The 20 tribes in the case area are diverse in many respects, although they share high unemployment rates, a strong sense of community, and a heavy dependence on fisheries. As many as 80 percent of the members of some tribes are dependent on fishing, either directly or through employment in tribal fisheries management programs. Many tribes are currently diversifying their economies by opening gaming casinos or other enterprises, but for the short term at least, fishing is the primary on-reservation economic activity for many tribes. The tribes range in size from a few hundred to several thousand members. Some tribes have a high proportion of non-Indians living on their reservations; others, particularly the more remote, coastal communities, are fairly homogeneous in terms of ethnicity.

While the tribes themselves differ, the regulatory challenges they face are similar in many respects. Successful management of a complex common-pool resource requires the formulation and implementation of a management plan that ensures sustainable patterns of resource utilization. Each step of this process involves transactions costs. Tribes have to search for information about the productivity, abundance, and prior harvest rates of stocks important to their particular regions.[4] Members of a tribe must bargain among themselves over overall goals, the trade-offs between utilization and conservation, and allocation between groups. Doing so involves learning about the preferences of other groups and developing mechanisms to increase the credibility of commitments. Compliance with fishing regulations must be monitored and enforced, and there must also be mechanisms to ensure accountability between decision makers and tribal members. Community management has both strengths and weaknesses with respect to how these transaction costs are met.

Research and Development of Management Plans

Given the hostile climate that prevailed after the Boldt decision, the tribes were understandably unwilling to rely on state-generated data with respect to stock abundance, long-term productivity, harvest predictions, and the like. And in many cases, either the state was not forthcoming with relevant information or the required data simply did not exist. The state had traditionally managed for aggregate yields, rather than individual stocks. Indi-

---

4. Some readers might wonder whether scientific or biological data should be considered a *transaction* cost or simply a cost like any other. Yet scientific information is not neutral; its potential to result in costs or benefits to particular parties is often what determines what information is generated and which set of estimates is used.

vidual tribes were interested in developing models of the stocks specific to their respective regions, since it was only these fish that they were entitled to catch.

While a few tribes already had professionally staffed fisheries departments in the early 1970s, most initially relied on the U.S. Fish and Wildlife Service to provide fisheries data. As the decision was implemented, federal funds became available to tribes seeking to develop their own fisheries departments. Tribes were then in a position to hire fisheries biologists, statisticians, and other professional staff. Today, most tribes have at least 10 fisheries department staff members; some of the larger tribes have as many as 30 staff members. Some tribes have formed management cooperatives in order to take advantage of economies of scale associated with some of the more specialized aspects of management. In addition, the Northwest Indian Fisheries Commission (NWIFC) generates systemwide information, and the two regional cooperatives provide their member tribes with data about their regions. The level of sophistication of the scientific modeling and technical information generated by the tribes is extremely high, particularly at the NWIFC and the two management cooperatives.

A typical staff would include a director of fisheries, several enhancement biologists, fisheries biologists, hatchery workers, one or more habitat biologists, fisheries enforcement officers, and various clerical and other support staff. Roughly half the members of a typical staff are professionals (James interview 1994). The majority of professionally trained staff members are non-Indians; tribal members are frequently employed in administrative support roles, as hatchery workers, or as enforcement officers. In most cases, salaries for biologists or other professionally trained staff are lower than they are for state workers in comparable positions, but this discrepancy has narrowed in recent years, at least for some tribes (Hage interview 1993). Jobs in the fisheries department are highly sought after by tribal members because they are relatively well paid and are often among the few reliable employment opportunities on the reservation. There is an informal but generally practiced rule that fishermen give up fishing while holding jobs in the fisheries department. Doing so reduces the potential of conflicts of interest while spreading economic opportunities more evenly throughout the tribe. About half the fisheries directors are tribal members, and the other half are professionally trained, non-Indian biologists.

While tribes were anxious to utilize the scientific and technical expertise of biologists and other professionals, they had no desire to become subject to a cadre of non-Indian professionals. The need to strike a balance between professional and technical expertise and tribal autonomy has produced an interesting configuration of institutional structures.

Directing the fisheries management staff are two, sometimes overlapping, regulatory bodies: the Fish Commissions or Committees and the Tribal Council.[5] The Tribal Council or equivalent is generally the final authority on fishing matters, and it generally must approve fishing regulations, capital projects, or fisheries-related litigation. Standing somewhere between the staff and the council in terms of its involvement with day-to-day decision making is the Fish Commission or Fish Committee, which is normally comprised of fishermen, either elected by their peers or appointed by the council from a list compiled by the fishermen.

Decision-Making Processes

There is considerable intertribal variation in the way decision-making authority is carved up between different structures. In theory, it is the job of the professional staff to interpret technical data, present management options to the Fish Commissions or Tribal Council or both, and implement their decisions by drafting appropriate regulations or undertaking particular enhancement projects. "Policy" decisions are to be made by a designated policy person, who might be the chair of the Fish Commission, a member of the staff, or, on important issues, a member of the tribal council. Actual practice reflects the fact that everything from the timing of a particular fishing opening to the tribe's bargaining position during annual preseason negotiations can be considered a policy issue. Since negotiations at the most important forums, such as the Pacific Salmon Treaty meetings and the Pacific Fishery Management Council meetings take place at a fairly elevated plane of technical knowledge, the professional staffs cannot avoid having influence over policy matters. Yet even if the distinction between technical and policy issues is occasionally blurred, the fact that it has been made explicit reminds the participants of their different roles in the process.

In most tribes, the Fish Commission makes all decisions concerning when fisheries are opened or closed, gear requirements, and the like. In some instances, decision making is fairly straightforward, because by the time the Fish Commission is making internal regulations, the options have been significantly narrowed during prior negotiation forums. At other times, the choices can be agonizing, such as when the Puyallup Fish Commission judged that opening a fishery on one species would endanger another and was forced to tell a group of waiting fishermen that a long-delayed fishery would be postponed yet again (Wright interview 1993). Or

---

5. In some tribes, the legislative body is the business council. To reduce confusion, I will refer to the legislative body of all tribes under discussion as the tribal council.

when the Nisqually Tribal Fish Commission, after an exceedingly poor year when there was little money in the community, voted to halt its bread-and-butter chum fishery one and one-half weeks prior to the peak of the run in order to avoid endangering a weak run of wild steelhead (Troutt interview 1993).

In other tribes, the Fish Commission or Committee merely sets general policy guidelines and leaves ongoing implementation to the fisheries director. This system is likely if (1) the tribe is fairly small or tribal leadership is stretched thin and (2) there is a long-standing relationship between the fisheries manager and the Fish Committee or Commission that allows the manager to anticipate their positions on nearly all issues. For example, neither the composition of the Fish Committee nor the fisheries manager at the Swinomish Tribe has changed since 1978. Both the fish committee members and the fisheries manager consider it unnecessary to have frequent meetings to cover long-settled issues, although the fisheries manager will call a meeting if she is unsure about the committee's position regarding an unforeseen issue (Loomis interview 1993).

Most tribal councils leave day-to-day management to the fish commissions and the fisheries staff, but the council will become involved if it considers that an issue concerns policy. Many tribes also enable the council to adjudicate serious disputes between the Fish Commission and the Fisheries staff, although such occasions are rare.[6] And like political bodies everywhere, a Tribal Council may chose to distance itself from the responsibility of making decisions that are certain to be divisive by placing the issue before the entire tribe. For example, the Port Gamble S'Klallam Tribe recently placed the issue of spousal fishing (whether nonmember spouses should have fishing rights) before all voting members of the tribe (Williams interview 1992).

In one style of management, the professional staff limits itself to presenting management options to the Fish Commission, which makes all decisions on opening and closing fisheries, gear restrictions, and the like. The staff's role is restricted to presenting technical data and implementing decisions made by the Fish Commission. From the point of view of the staff, this approach has some advantages because it insulates them from the political heat that can accompany a decision on a politically unpopular or divisive issue (Troutt interview 1993). In other tribes, the fisheries department staffs take a somewhat more activist approach, particularly in small tribes or in tribes where fishing opportunities are relatively poor.

It is normal for Fish Commission decisions to be made by consensus,

---

6. These disputes are very infrequent, but when they occur, they are likely to involve conservation issues. Since it is slightly more insulated from pressure by fishermen, the council is more likely to make a decision that reflects the long-term interests of the tribe.

although few have rules that require it. At first glance, that would appear to be a source of high transaction costs, but a closer look indicates a more complicated story. While often time-consuming to achieve, a consensually reached decision is invested with an added measure of authority. Consensus is often used as a decision rule in situations where a governing body is also responsible for implementation or where the group's capacities to enforce a rule are limited (Bailey 1965). Similarly, consensus decision making may be efficient where monitoring and enforcement costs are potentially very high.

Consensus decision making also minimizes the amount of blame that can be placed on individual decision makers in the event of an unpopular decision, and it is this factor that probably explains why tribal decision-making forums tend to employ it. A perhaps unintended but nonetheless beneficial consequence of such a rule is that it reduces the short-term bias that frequently characterizes decision making by elected officials. If fish commissioners make decisions as a body, individual decision makers are granted more latitude to consider the long-term effects of policies. With respect to high transaction costs associated with protracted discussion and negotiation, it is not clear what value should be placed on expenditures of time where the opportunity costs for that time are relatively low, for example, in situations such as exist in most tribal fisheries where the available fishing days are few in number. That is not to say that tribal fish commissioners, like anyone else, do not become frustrated with protracted discussions. It does seem plausible, however, that where the costs of having unreconciled differences are high and the opportunity costs of time spent in discussion are relatively low, a consensus rule would be likely to emerge.

Monitoring and Enforcement

A viable management plan requires credible monitoring and enforcement mechanisms. While a few tribes had robust regulatory regimes in place throughout the 20th century, for most, creating them was a formidable undertaking. The situation was complicated by strong antiregulatory sentiment. The only experience most tribal members had had with fisheries law enforcement was with state Fish and Game department wardens. During the long campaign leading up to the Boldt decision, illegal fishing was infused with the rectitude of civil disobedience. Confrontations between fishermen and enforcement agents had provided some of the most compelling media coverage of the whole issue of Northwest tribal treaty rights. Not surprisingly, the immediate reaction of many tribal fishermen to the Boldt decision was to resist any attempts to contain their fishing opportunities. For many tribal fishermen, being limited to specific areas (UAPs) appeared overly restrictive relative to past practices or to what some thought the treaties had promised. Moreover, illegal fishing among non-treaty fishermen was rampant throughout the mid- to late 1970s. Establishing the legitimacy of tribal regulation and enforcement was a difficult, yet essential, task.

Not only was the regulatory climate unpromising, but tribes often lacked legal infrastructure such as well-developed legal codes, prosecutors, and judges. Even those individuals who would have been prepared to cooperate had they received assurances that others were doing so were unlikely to comply under these circumstances. Yet for many of the tribes, especially the smaller, recently organized, or poorer ones, the costs of constructing a full-fledged system of enforcement and adjudication would have been prohibitive. In 1979, 15 of the tribes formed the Northwest Intertribal Court System (NICS), which provides legal infrastructure to its member tribes. NICS is funded through the BIA. The most immediate goal of the tribes was to make enforcement of fishing regulations credible. This goal was accomplished through the creation of a circuit court system in which judges, prosecutors, and, until recently, defense attorneys traveled to the different reservations to adjudicate cases.[7] The enforcement staff and a tribal clerk of the court do the initial processing of cases. NICS also hears cases regarding housing, law and order, and other matters.

In 1981, NICS also began providing code writing services. Part of the impetus behind this addition was that many ordinances and tribal legal codes were vague enough so that the successful prosecution of violations was proving to be difficult, which undermined public confidence in the reliability and predictability of judicial outcomes. As the tribes and NICS became more experienced, that became less of a problem. Refinement and greater precision of tribal codes is an ongoing objective of NICS, but recently code writers have also begun a project of developing alternatives to Anglo-American traditional forms of justice. These "alternative courts," based on what are believed to be aboriginal practices, use NICS-trained tribal mediators to resolve damage claims or other private disputes. According to code writers at NICS, tribal mediators are often able to provide a more satisfactory resolution to disputes because they are able to talk directly with the parties about problems that underlie a specific dispute (Bohl interview 1994). As tribes continue to grow, some are opting to operate their own judicial systems, but it is likely that at least the smaller tribes will continue to find membership in NICS attractive on the grounds of economies of scale.

---

7. Budget cuts have necessitated discontinuing public defender services.

Strengths and Weaknesses of Community-Based Enforcement

A small-scale, community-based system of regulation and enforcement reduces many of the transaction costs associated with enforcement, although it may increase others. Tribal law and order codes and fisheries codes are adopted after considerable public discussion and comment. Public awareness of regulations or changes in regulations is generally high. And since tribal codes are written by community members themselves (with the assistance of attorneys), great pains are taken to ensure that the language is plain and direct (Bohl interview 1994). Furthermore, as some social scientists have suggested, willingness to comply with rules seems to be greater when users participate in the process of crafting them (Ostrom 1990). The experience of many tribal fisheries seems to bear that out. At the Sauk-Suiattle Tribe, where members of the Fish Commission write their own regulations, as they do in most tribal fisheries, tribal fisheries manager Lawrence Joseph explains, "Right now we don't have too many tickets. Because it is a standard that's acceptable among all the fishermen. It's their social standards about how they would handle themselves" (Joseph interview 1992).

Second, tribal communities can and do exercise the power to shun or ostracize rule violators (Bohl interview 1994). Their capacity to do so is based on the high level of interdependence and interrelatedness between members. While tribal communities are far less interdependent than they once were—tribal members are more likely to depend on government transfer payments or outside employment for income than upon each other—their relations with one another are multifaceted and pivotal to social and economic well-being in a way they are not in many non-Indian settings, at least not in the urban and suburban neighborhoods where most individuals live. In the course of everyday life, most tribal members rely on a considerable amount of mutual aid; when someone's car breaks down or a family loses its possessions in a house fire, he or she can normally count on the assistance of others. That is not to say that relations between individuals are universally friendly; in fact, it is precisely the fact that people are expected to extend aid to others even if they don't like them that demonstrates the relative strength of community bonds (Taylor 1982).

Like neighbors in small towns, people living on Indian reservations know a great deal about what others are up to. The omnipresence and apparent omniscience of one's neighbors is so powerful that it has given rise to its own rueful genre of humor. Whatever positive or negative contribution this pervasive scrutiny makes to the overall quality of community life, it has the potential to lower monitoring costs. Tribal fishermen are nearly always aware of who is fishing against regulations, and if they consider the infraction to be serious, they will usually take steps to discipline the person themselves or report the offender to an enforcement officer (Sele interview 1993). Community members not only know what others are doing at present, but they usually can recite the salient features of a particular individual's life history, or at least that of his or her family. Whereas most Americans move several times in the course of a lifetime, many Indians live and die among the same, relatively small group of people. Reputation matters in practical, mundane ways that it often does not for people who live in more porous, mobile communities.

Knowing about a rule violation is not the same as doing something about it. Whether informal sanctioning takes place is partly determined by the nature of the offense. Tribal fishermen are more likely to consider violations as serious and warranting action if they are involve conservation issues. Tribal legal codes also reflect the perception of the seriousness of conservation offenses. Particularly if another fishermen's illegal acts are perceived as conservation related or as directly benefiting him at a cost to the larger group of fishermen, some form of sanctioning is likely to follow. One low-cost, very effective, and widely used method is to publicize the offense and the identity of the offender over the short-wave radio. The fisheries manager for the Jamestown S'Klallam Tribe reports that it is not uncommon to hear messages such as "Did you see so-and-so flying all that net?" over the short-wave frequency—a clear reference to a violation of specified gear limits. Since all fishermen listen to their short-wave radios constantly, such publicity is tantamount to erecting a flashing neon sign over the boat of the offender. Such treatment might be preceded or followed by a direct approach to the rule violator, advising him to resolve the problem. In some tribes, a group of fishermen might delegate themselves to speak to the person. If none of the preceding methods worked, the rule violator would be reported to tribal enforcement staff. Generally, tribal fishermen prefer to try to resolve such problems themselves before reporting them to enforcement personnel.

Trying to establish or compare levels of noncompliance within or between state and tribal fisheries is a nearly impossible task, since the level of known violations is to a large extent an artifact of the amount of effort devoted to looking for them. Nonetheless, the evidence that does exist suggests that compliance with fishing regulations has improved dramatically over the last twenty years (Pinkerton and Keitlah 1990, Mathews interview 1993). While the increased credibility of formal institutions for monitoring and enforcement have contributed to that, the increased legitimacy that has accompanied self-regulation has played at least as large a role. As one tribal manager states,

The laws and policies are just signposts anyway. It's got to be within the heart or mind of the people to make the law work. If it's not in their mind or not in their heart, you'd have to have an army out there to keep everybody under control. (Joseph interview 1992)

At the same time, the system of community monitoring and enforcement that is present on many reservations is not a panacea for solving all social order or even all fishing violation problems. It is not, for example, sufficiently robust to deal with particularly recalcitrant individuals or those who are impervious to the threat of a withdrawal of mutual aid or social approval. Whether it was once, when tribal communities were stronger, is at least arguable, but tribal members are currently either unwilling or unable to resort to the kind of strong sanctions that would be required in these cases where informal sanctioning is inadequate, preferring to rely on formal monitoring systems. The fact that in these cases tribal enforcement officers (and for some purposes, state enforcement officers as well) take action against alleged violators is not a situation people are interested in altering.[8] Since the formal monitoring and enforcement system is a low-cost alternative that is readily available to them, this is not surprising.

In some cases, the very features that make informal systems work well in many situations incapacitate them in others. For example, violations classified as criminal, which include some fishing offenses, require a jury trial. The small size of the population would mean that most members of the jury pool are likely to be either related to or involved in some type of direct and continuing interaction with the accused or some member of his or her family. The result has been that it has been very difficult to find juries willing to convict offenders. Tribes are currently investigating the possibility of pooling the jury pools of several tribes or inviting nontribal members to serve on juries in tribal court (Bohl interview 1994).

The relative ease with which members of such a close-knit community can communicate and reach agreements can facilitate *non*compliance in some circumstances. One tribal manager reports that it would not be unusual for a tribal fisherman to fail to report an observed violation if he either had committed or expected to commit a similar offense (Jorgenson interview 1994). A pattern of silence in the face of observed offenses would be particularly likely to emerge in the event that there was a low probability that violators would be caught or punished. In this instance, then, hav-

---

8. Most tribes have agreements with the Washington Department of Fisheries that allow Washington Department of Fisheries patrol officers to detain a tribal member who is violating tribal regulations until tribal personnel arrive to cite him. Tribal officers can do the same with nontreaty fishermen (Mathews interview 1993).

ing a credible formal enforcement system reinforces informal systems of control.

Allocating the Benefits to the Fishery

Deciding how to share the benefits of the fishery and setting overall goals for its development requires considerable discussion and bargaining between tribal members. Even apparently straightforward fishing regulations concerning the timing and length of openings are never neutral with respect to distribution. As the tribal fisheries have become more crowded, allocating fishing opportunities between different types of fishermen has become more difficult. Tribal fisheries are unusually diverse, covering the spectrum from traditional river fishermen to those with large gillnet or purse seine boats who appear indistinguishable from their nontreaty counterparts. While a few tribes such as the Nisqually fish only in the river, using methods not too dissimilar from those of their forebears, most tribes must balance the needs of their set net and skiff fishermen (the small-boat fishermen) with those of the highly efficient, mobile large boat fleet (the large-boat fishermen).

In the tribes where there are these cleavages, they tend to reflect differences in wealth, skill, and experience. Most fishermen began fishing in the river with a small skiff. The more successful ones have gradually acquired enough capital to buy a boat large enough to fish the marine waters. In recent years, it has become far more difficult to make enough money to move up through the ranks. Younger fishermen and those who have been less successful either at fishing or at acquiring good business skills remain in the small-boat fishery, where they are subject to prior interceptions of fish by fishermen in larger boats.

Potential distributional conflicts exist both between and among fishermen using different types of gear. For example, set net fishermen fish at fixed sites, which in some tribes are considered hereditary property. Sites vary in terms of their productivity. Along the Nisqually River, for instance, fishermen with sites in the lower end of a river generally do much better than those in the upper end. The Nisqually Fish Commission has in the past attempted to resolve the distributional problems this difference in sites creates by staggering two-day openings for the upper-end and river fishermen, but it has since discontinued the practice because it carries the risk of not catching the fish at all (Troutt interview 1993).

At the Port Gamble S'Klallam Tribe, there is no tradition of family ownership, and there is competition between fishermen for the best sites in Port Gamble Bay. Some years ago, the tribe devised a means to allocate sites. At the beginning of the season, the names of all eligible fishers are placed in a hat, and a child picks names to determine initial site locations.

Once a week, each fishermen moves five sites forward.[9] In most years, the season lasts long enough so that at least one rotation around Port Gamble Bay is possible and each fisher gets a chance at both favorable and unfavorable locations (Williams interview 1992). Another lottery is used to allocate shellfish gathering days. In some tribes, the rule is simply first come, first served, and fishermen will put their skiff next to a desired site 24 hours or more prior to an opening. Among members of the Hoh Tribe, it is written into the fishing ordinances that disputes over sites will be handled by drawing straws (Bohl interview 1994).

The large, commercial power gillnet and purse seine boat fishermen fish mainly in the marine waters of Puget Sound, where open competition is the formal rule. Nonetheless, under an informal agreement, tribal managers attempt to obtain a 40–60 division between purse seines and gillnet boats.[10] This division is accomplished through adjusting the timing of an opening—a 6:00 a.m. opening favors purse seiners; a 6:00 p.m. opening favors gillnetters. Or if the objective is to allocate more fish to smaller gillnet boats (as it often is), a manager might extend the amount of fishing time but schedule it before or after the run is expected to peak. Doing so reduces the risk that the highly efficient purse seine and large gillnet boats will take the allowable catch in the space of one short opening, leaving no opportunity for the smaller boats to make more than one landing (Loomis interview 1993). It also reduces the incentives to fishermen in smaller boats to attempt to bring in more fish than they can safely carry.

When there is a fishing opening in the "outside" marine waters, the big-boat fishermen are expected to stay out of the more sheltered bays and riverine areas fished by the small-boat fishermen. In some tribes this is a formal rule, in others it is simply an understanding. The fact that it is nearly always observed may be attributable more to self-interest than self-restraint, since the fishing is generally better in the outside waters. The objective of this rule is to give opportunities to different types of fishermen, although it is to some extent canceled out by the fact that most tribes allow fishermen to license more than one boat, which means that an individual can move from one boat to another in order to participate in more openings.

Underlying Principles for Allocation

Although tribes stop short of setting quotas by gear type, they use the aforementioned and other methods to allocate the benefits of the fishery

---

9. A similar lottery system for allocating fishing sites is in place in at least one artisanal fishery in Turkey (Ostrom 1990, Berkes 1986).

10. This split applies mainly to the North Sound tribes, which fish the very lucrative Fraser River sockeye runs headed for Canada. The South Sound and terminal-area tribes do not have purse seine boats.

between competing groups. The universal underlying principle or decision rule as articulated by fisheries managers and fish commissions is that each group should receive a "fair" opportunity to fish. Yet there is no obvious definition of what constitutes fairness, given the very different levels of investment (and thus the necessary return) for the different gear types. In practice, "fairness" is interpreted to mean that no qualified group of fishermen should be excluded from participating in the fishery and that the pattern of intergroup distribution should remain relatively constant from year to year.

It is considered the responsibility of the Fish Commission to make regulatory decisions that are consistent with what fishermen believe is fair. Tribes like the Lummi, which were the first to experience rapid, uneven growth in their fisheries, have experimented with different ways of ensuring that the interests of different groups are represented in the decision-making process. One early method was to designate roughly half the positions on the Fish Commission for representatives of particular gear types. The result was high levels of conflict. It appears that designating seats by gear type caused the holders of those seats to become more intransigent and less willing to compromise. Individuals interpreted their role to be almost entirely one of representing their constituents, without regard for the general interest. After several years of turmoil and divisiveness, they discontinued this system in favor of direct election of candidates by list.

Under the current system of direct election used by the Lummi tribes, there is no guarantee that gear-type groups will be proportionally represented.[11] There is, however, a very strong norm that Fish Commissioners are to be evenhanded and refrain from favoring members of their own gear group. Weighing the interests of all groups is made easier by the fact that many small-boat fishermen alternate between working on a large seiner as a crew member (for which they generally are paid by share) and fishing from their own small skiff when the outside waters are closed. Somewhat less compelling but certainly not trivial is the fact that owners of large boats generally have younger relatives in the small-boat fishery in the river where they themselves began fishing. Fishermen use gossip, name-calling (often via short-wave radio), and other forms of social sanctioning to discipline Fish Commissioners who are perceived to be favoring their own group.

All tribes prioritize ceremonial and subsistence uses over commercial fishing, although the line separating subsistence from commercial fishing is not always clear, especially when fishing is poor. Small-boat fishermen are

---

11. Many of the tribes use staggered terms of election and select the requisite number of top vote getters. In some tribes, the Tribal Council appoints the Fish Committee, while in others there is an election after which the Tribal Council retains the power to approve the top vote getters.

considered commercial fishermen, although in many tribes, they are for all practical purposes fishing for subsistence use because of the paucity of fish. Tribes make an effort to spread the benefits of the fishery throughout the tribe, even among those who do not fish. On the Swinomish reservation, for example, elderly tribal members receive a weekly fish dinner. At most tribes, fish for weddings, funerals, and other ceremonies are caught each year by a group of volunteer commercial fishermen and then frozen and parceled out as the need arises. A fairly typical description of the underlying principles of allocation decisions is the following:

> [N]umber one, get the escapement in the river, number two, provide for any ceremonial uses within the tribe, number three, provide subsistence opportunity, number four, be reasonable about the way you allocate commercial opportunity—don't lock any particular fishery out and make sure everybody gets their fair share. (Sele interview 1993)

Assessing Tribal Management

It is clear that tribal management structures are quite successful in using the comparative advantages they possess with respect to various aspects of the management process.[12] Their system of monitoring and enforcement combines the strengths of informal and formal structures in a system that is remarkably successful, given the inherent difficulties and the historical circumstances that existed at the onset of self-management. The tripartite structure of staff, fishermen, and tribal council emphasizes participation and ensures that the power to make important decisions remains in the hands of tribal members, yet it incorporates the knowledge and technical expertise of professionally trained scientists. The network of regional and intertribal management structures that has emerged allows tribes to take advantage of economies of scale in areas where they exist, yet retains a great deal of authority at the local level. At the same time, a puzzling question remains. The average income of a tribal fishermen has significantly declined over time, partly because of increases in the numbers of fishermen.[13] By limiting the number of fishermen in each fishery, tribes could reduce overcrowding and actual or potential overcapitalization problems. Yet with a few exceptions, they do not. Is this simply a failure to solve a collective action problem or is there something more complicated going on?

---

12. Pinkerton and Keitlah (1990) reach a similar conclusion with respect to the Point No Point Treaty Council, the management consortium of the four tribes along the Straits of Juan de Fuca and Hood Canal.

13. Declining fish prices are also responsible for diminished incomes.

Why Tribes Seldom Limit Entry

It is not entirely accurate to say that tribes do not limit entry. Over time, there has clearly been an evolution toward stricter requirements governing who can fish. With the exception of nonmember spouses, for whom some tribes make an exception, all tribes now limit fishing rights to tribal members.[14] Most tribes have a blood quantum requirement for membership of one-quarter, although in a few tribes it is one-eighth. Some tribes limit fishing rights to those tribal members who reside on the reservation. One tribe limits participation to one fishermen per family. Most tribes have adopted measures aimed at retaining the benefits of the fishery within the tribe. For example, in the early years when few tribal members had enough capital to invest in boats, nontreaty fishermen would lease boats to treaty fishermen for a share of the profits. As time has gone on, most tribes have banned or strongly discouraged this practice. And in an effort to reduce overcapitalization, the four Point No Point Treaty Council tribes have banned purse seine boats (the largest, most expensive, and most effective boats) within the areas they jointly regulate. Nonetheless, most tribal managers acknowledge that few fishermen are able to make a living at fishing and that gear is idle much of the season.

There are three competing or overlapping stories that can be told to explain why tribes fail to limit entry. The first is based on the economic self-interests of tribes vis-à-vis other tribes. It would be irrational for any particular tribe to limit entry unless other tribes are also prepared to limit entry or tribes have secured shares. Nearly all tribal managers mention this argument as one obstacle to a limited-entry program (Loomis interview 1993; James interview 1994). If that is the reason for the failure to limit entry, then this situation should not be construed as an unsolved internal collective action because there is no alternative that could make the group better off. In the case of at least one tribe, in which a fisheries manager counseled a tribal council not to proceed with limiting entry because of intertribal considerations, that may have been a determining factor (Lampsakis interview 1993). In most tribes, however, there appear to be other, probably more important, elements to this decision.

The second explanation stems from what would be rational for the individual fishermen with respect to internal competition. Most fishermen oppose a limited-entry program, and it is commonly accepted wisdom among fish commissioners and fisheries managers and tribal council mem-

---

14. The issue of nonmember spousal fishing is very controversial, both within and between tribes. The fisheries manager of one tribe that does allow the practice points out that such a rule affects men and women differently. Since fishing remains a male-dominated occupation, it is far more likely to be a female tribal member who must hire someone from outside her family to fish in her boat than a male (Loomis interview 1993).

bers that to attempt to introduce such a measure would be political suicide. As one fisheries staff member puts it, "We wouldn't touch that with a ten-foot pole" (Davis interview 1993). Much of the opposition could be interpreted as stemming from a fear that instituting a limited-entry program would make some individuals worse off. In other words, fishermen fear that they (or their children) run the risk of being excluded from the fishery or that the economic benefits to limiting entry will not be redistributed. This fear is a common obstacle to solving the bargaining problem that is a part of achieving cooperation in (almost all) collective action problems.[15]

Yet people express their opposition to limited-entry programs quite differently, which brings up the third explanation. Fishermen and fish commissioners explain their opposition to limiting entry by saying that fishing is a tribal right and that a limited-entry program is therefore prohibited. That is a false belief, since there are no legal grounds that would prevent a tribe from regulating its fishermen in this way. In fact, one tribe has always limited entry to its fisheries,[16] and all the tribes exercise their authority by regulating their fishermen in some ways. At the same time, this notion of fishing as an inalienable right possessed by all tribal members seems to be indicative of something more than an elaborate self-deception or a mask for simple economic self-interest.

The acts of fishing and of managing fisheries are powerful expressions of a distinct social identity. They evoke a distant past when Indian people were secure and self-sufficient, as well as a heroic struggle against a large and powerful external force. Fishing was the most important traditional activity of Northwest coastal Indians, and participation in the modern fishery, even if it only occurs episodically, conveys a sense of cultural continuity.[17] That explains why in many tribes, participation itself is a primary goal of fisheries management. In some tribes, the value placed on participation extends to creating an unstated long-term goal of discouraging anyone from trying to make a living at fishing, in lieu of providing an opportunity for all tribal members to fish (Troutt 1993). Allocative efficiency in the sense of maximizing overall profits is simply not an important goal for many tribal managers.

---

15. Gary Libecap (1989) identifies bargaining problems, especially in situations with heterogeneous users, as the primary obstacle to solutions to problems associated with common-pool resources.

16. The Quinaults, who live on a large reservation along an isolated section of the Washington coast, have operated a limited-entry fishery for many years. Its existence is at least partly a result of the fact that the Quinaults have had unusually strong, stable leadership and there are employment opportunities on the reservation in addition to fishing.

17. Any conversation with Indian fishermen about fishing invariably evokes references to the past, such as "My grandfather fished in this same stretch of river," or to their desire to create fishing opportunities for their children.

This contrast of goals can be illustrated by the marked difference in the way the concept of limited entry is interpreted by some tribal fisheries managers and economists. For an economist, designing a limited entry program involves determining the number of boats needed to take the harvestable fish and then designating the optimal number of spots to particular fishermen by some preestablished rule. Doing so can be expected to maximize allocative efficiency because it minimizes overcapitalization. For most tribal fishermen or fisheries managers, the goal of a limited-entry program is assumed to be that of making sure everyone who wants to can participate (Troutt interview 1993). Thus, limiting entry means limiting each fishermen to one boat or one net, or limiting the net size of each boat. Any of these are regulatory actions that run counter to what efficiency would suggest.

Many tribal fishermen barely break even through fishing. In some years, they operate at a loss. Yet the idea of selling fishing rights is anathema to them. When posed with the hypothetical question of whether they would be prepared to stop fishing if offered an equivalent amount of money to stay home, their reactions are vehemently negative.[18] Tribal fishermen represent themselves as having an innate relationship with and responsibility to the salmon resource, which sets them apart from other (non-Indian) fishermen. This is not to say that tribal fishermen are unconcerned with internal or intertribal competition or other issues that have a direct effect on their economic interests. They clearly do, and the evolution of internal institutions of fisheries management reflects their efforts to grapple with these issues. But viewing the incentives operating on tribal fishermen and tribal managers strictly through the lenses of thin rationality does not touch on some important parts of the story.

---

18. One tribal fisherman, who was fishing in a small boat and could not conceivably have grossed more than $5,000 a year, replied to the female interviewer that if a man had asked him that question, he would have hit him (Anonymous Squaxin Island fisherman 1993).

Conclusion

In the introduction to this book, I raised two interrelated questions. The first concerned whether, contra Garrett Hardin and other adherents of the "tragedy of the commons" model, user groups can effectively manage natural resource systems. More specifically, I wanted to use the case of a large, complicated, transboundary natural resource system to expand on recent work concerning local management of common-pool resources. I wanted to see the effects of combining a number of small-scale, participatory decision-making bodies with what had been a politically centralized, traditional state management agency. One practical goal of this study, then, was to assess the strengths and weaknesses of comanagement and determine its potential contribution to the successful management of other common-pool resources.

The second question concerns the kind of institutions emerging from this complicated system of multilayered bargaining and decision making. Are the institutions that are created at each of these three levels—state-tribal, intertribal, and intratribal—effective in helping the relevant groups solve collective action problems? In the language of transaction costs, with the help of these institutions, are groups of individuals able to solve the problems they face by minimizing (1) transaction costs and (2) deadweight losses arising from failures to exploit potential gains from trade? What principles do these institutions appear to represent? And finally, what does the process of their emergence and evolution tell us about institutions and institutional change more generally? I turn now to these questions.

The Potential of Comanagement

Successful management of a common-pool resource (CPR) involves solving a series of collective action problems. One of the most important of these is that the regulators must create and enforce rules that result in sustainable patterns of use of the resource. Work on local management of common-pool resources indicates that for a self-governing community to successfully manage a common-pool resource, it must (1) have incentives to conserve (that is, it must be rational for it to do so) and (2) have the capacity to overcome collective action problems. Both are necessary conditions. Clearly, the first condition is more likely to be satisfied if the resource system in question is relatively small and well bounded, which increases the likelihood that the benefits of the group's self-restraint cannot be usurped by outsiders. The second condition is more likely to be met if the group is relatively small, has a stable membership, and is fairly homogeneous. Most research on locally managed CPRs has been confined to cases where both the resource system and the group are small. For example, Elinor Ostrom's well-known study of 15 common pool resource management situations focuses exclusively on such cases (Ostrom 1990, 26).

The situation I have described is quite different. The Pacific salmon fisheries are a large, transboundary resource, and a great many highly heterogeneous groups use the resource. The fish travel long distances and are affected by habitat conditions across a wide area. Any particular user group or tribe is faced with considerable uncertainty with respect to what others are doing at present or are likely to do, and regarding how the legal rules governing harvest management or alteration of fish habitat may change. *Unconditional* conservation would not be rational under these circumstances. In other words, any individual user group or tribe is unlikely to find it in its interests to *unilaterally* (1) exercise collective self-restraint and (2) pay the costs of collecting information and monitoring and enforcing regulations. Thus, if the users are rational and if the economic benefits of the fishery are the only things they are interested in, they would be unlikely to conserve.

If a group can be provided with assurances that others are cooperating (conserving), however, then conservation may be a rational strategy for any particular community of users. Thus, allowing the state to perform an oversight role with respect to conservation for all user groups may be rational for any particular group, particularly if they have recourse to an appeal process in the event that the state fails to respect their authority or fails to apply standards evenhandedly. In this case, the federal court and the dispute resolution process established by the court fulfill that role. States can also collect information about the actions and preferences of far-flung users and coordinate the information gathered about conditions affecting salmon along their migratory paths. States, supratribal organizations, and other regulatory bodies such as the Pacific Fishery Management Council and the various panels that make up the Pacific Salmon Treaty contribute to successful management largely through stabilizing expectations and facilitating the cooperation of a large number of disparate groups, rather than relying solely on top-down command and control.

Local communities have a number of strengths that state resource management agencies typically lack. The high cost of obtaining various sorts of information is a major problem for any centralized approach to resource management (Baland and Plateau 1996; Shelley et al. 1996, Wilson et al. 1994). As demonstrated in chapter 6, cohesive communities can substantially reduce the costs of monitoring and enforcement. Local communities are also in a better position to gather place-specific information about conditions affecting the movement of stocks and broader issues affecting salmon ecology. Furthermore, while state agencies have traditionally been primarily interested in maximizing aggregate yields, local user groups can be expected to take a greater interest in the individual stocks that comprise the building blocks of the system.

In the Pacific Northwest comanagement regime, this heightened interest is unquestionably present since each tribe's fishing rights are spatially delineated and thus specific to particular stocks. As we saw in chapter 4, tribes, particularly those that fish primarily in the rivers, are interested in protecting "their" stocks until they arrive in tribal fishing areas. The state, on the other hand, faces high opportunity costs in protecting weak stocks because doing so necessitates forgoing, or at least postponing, the opportunity to harvest the intermingled large, healthy runs. The fact that each side has the authority to check the other as well as the incentive to do so at the very point in the process where the other's will to conserve is likely to falter is a critical element of the viability of this system. The net effect is to include in the decision-making process a fairly large number of groups whose heterogeneous interests can be backed up with defendable claims. The result should be greater protection of biodiversity. A recent study of the health of wild salmon stocks in California and the Pacific Northwest demonstrated that while wild stocks are in jeopardy throughout their range, 64 of the 99 remaining healthy native stocks are in Washington State (Huntington, Nehlsen, and Bowers 1996). Nonetheless, there is simply too little evidence and there are too many variables affecting salmon to state categorically that comanagement has had this effect.

State agencies and local communities bring to the management process a very different set of skills and interests. In the comanagement regime I have described, in some respects the parties have been able to utilize their comparative advantages in various aspects of the management process, and the result has been a productive division of labor. The line between useful checks and balances and inefficient duplication of efforts is not always observed, however. In the areas of data collection, statistical modeling, and run-size predictions, initial asymmetries of information and a lack of trust have often produced a duplication, rather than cooperation.

The system may currently reflect overinvestments in research, data collection, and statistical modeling capacity.[1] To some extent this duplication may be inevitable. A large part of what makes this system work is that the different parties have the capability as well as the authority to practice mutual oversight. Nonetheless, the fact that over time there has been increasing specialization of effort and sharing of various management tasks suggests that if mutual trust continues to develop, efficiency will continue to improve as well.

One beneficial consequence of having two sets of biologists, statisticians, and other scientists who perform similar tasks is that Indian fishermen appear to be far more familiar with and willing to accept the findings of scientists than are fishermen in traditionally managed systems. Distrust of scientists and of the techniques used in generating the data used by managers to set regulations is endemic among fishermen, which tends to undermine the effectiveness of the management system in a variety of ways. Particularly in an environment where monitoring and enforcement are costly and therefore limited, the effectiveness of regulations is greatly affected by individuals' beliefs about the nature of the problem and whether they think a proposed solution or set of regulations addresses it correctly. The problem (and the likelihood of opportunistic behavior) is exacerbated by the existence of a plethora of potential threats to the sustainability of resource systems. Fishermen and other resource users often claim, either strategically or sincerely, that their actions are not to blame for problems with the maintenance of various sorts of renewable resources systems; that such problems are either (1) greatly exaggerated or (2) due to some cause other than their own actions.[2] In the comanagement system described here, the credibility of biologists and other scientists is enhanced among Indian fishermen by the fact that they are employed by the tribes, rather

---

1. On the other hand, an unintended consequence of the comanagement regime is that there has been a significant research effort devoted to understanding the complications of salmon ecology in the Pacific Northwest. If we assume that the short-term bias that tends to dominate the calculations of elected officials generally results in an *underinvestment* in environmental research, this is a useful corrective.

2. A spectacular, although by no means unusual, demonstration of this pattern of distrust and denial can be seen in the events leading up to the recent collapse of what has been for at least 300 years one of the greatest fisheries in the world, New England's Georges Banks. As the authors of a recent article state, "For years, there has been open hostility between groundfishermen and the fisheries scientists who have been evaluating groundfish stock conditions. As the foregoing account . . . illustrates repeatedly, scientific advice was routinely ignored by the Council and the region's fishermen who did not see what the scientists were seeing and did not understand the implications of what the scientists were saying" (Shelley et al. 1996, 242).

than the state. In addition, professionally trained fisheries scientists work closely with the Indian fish committee members (who are often fishermen themselves) and with other tribal member–employees in executing day-to-day management tasks. This close working relationship creates an environment in which scientific information is disseminated in such a way as to make it credible to fishermen, who are then more likely to comply with regulations premised on scientists' recommendations.

In conclusion, comanagement is initially quite costly but has considerable potential to enhance the effectiveness of a resource management regime. It requires significant outlays of time spent in gathering new information and in negotiating agreements. At the same time, if the process is successful, it reduces monitoring and enforcement costs by increasing the legitimacy of the system of management. Having such a system may encourage people to overachieve by voluntarily contributing to the preservation and protection of the resource. There is also a scientific basis for comanagement. It is the current view among fisheries scientists that the biological environment of fisheries is extremely complex and not well understood (Ludwig, Hilborn, and Wallace 1993; Wilson et al. 1994). There is a critical need to collect more data about subtle changes in the small and varied areas of marine and freshwater that together comprise the larger biological community. Comanagement seems to have a natural comparative advantage in supplying that sort of information.

Do the lessons of this comanagement system have wider applicability? At first glance, it seems to be a highly unusual resource system and set of circumstances. But appearances deceive. There are a considerable number of large, transboundary environmental resources in the world, and most of them are poorly managed. Many of them are similarly complex biologically, have overlapping jurisdictions, and have complicated and often conflictual relationships between various user groups and between user groups and managers. Giving greater authority to local communities and encouraging state actors to specialize in facilitating and coordinating agreements reached by the relevant parties (i.e., to act as political entrepreneurs) rather than simply through top-down structures of authority is an approach to resource management that is deserving of further investigation. For migratory or very large resource systems in particular, encouraging a more federated system of problem solving, but one backed up by a centralized authority, seems desirable.

Small, bounded resource systems (common pastures, forests, and the like) may in many situations benefit from a cooperative state and local management regime as well. Local communities throughout the world, many of which have managed resources sustainably for hundreds of years, are increasingly being threatened by population pressures from within and encroachment from without. Furthermore, such resource systems often contain attributes that are public goods to a larger collectivity. State or regional political bodies may be in the best position to represent the interests of these larger collectivities.

The fact that state agencies can function in this way does not, of course, mean that they will. As the history of state involvement in this fishery prior to 1974 demonstrates, the state's Department of Fish and Wildlife has traditionally been held captive by, on the one hand, a powerful commercial fishing industry, with the result that the resource was overcapitalized and overfished; and on the other, by a state legislature that was consistently willing to sacrifice native salmon runs and the protection of natural ecosystems to economic development. In addition, state fisheries managers strongly resisted sharing management responsibilities with the tribes. Without forceful action by the courts and the strong, skillful leadership provided by a new director of the state Department of Fisheries in the mid-1980s, the tribes and the state might still be locked in unproductive conflict.

Comanagement and incorporation of greater user-group participation into the management process more generally are currently very popular ideas among development specialists and natural resource management policy analysts. Yet while the Pacific Northwest system of tribal-state comanagement is by most accounts a success, user-group participation should not be seen as a panacea to the problems of managing natural resource systems. The state-tribal comanagement regime described here represents a quite radical devolution of decision-making authority. It is possible that trying to incorporate relatively limited participation into an otherwise traditional management regime may increase user groups' access to the decision-making process without conveying any enhanced sense of responsibility or accountability.[3] Moreover, it may lack the sort of mechanisms that allow the various actors to check and balance each other's interests. On the other hand, common-pool resources, particularly those that involve large, transboundary resource systems, are extremely difficult to manage sustainably. There may be no set of institutional arrangements that will prove to be entirely satisfactory. Comanagement systems are costly and far from perfect, but as is sometimes said about democracy itself, the alternatives have been shown, in most cases, to be even worse.

---

3. Some, although not all, of the regional councils operating under the Magnuson Fishery Conservation and Management Act appear to be vulnerable to this problem.

Institutions and Institutional Change

The second set of questions posed at the onset of this study concerned the character of the rules or governance structures that organized cooperation and conflict within and between three sets of actors and what the process of developing those rules indicates about institutions and institutional change. Do these institutions allow parties to minimize transaction costs and realize potential gains from cooperation? If they are *very* effective at this, and we make the standard rational choice assumptions about the actors' goals, we would expect the content of such rules to reflect allocative efficiency.

Chapters 4, 5, and 6 were each devoted to a different set of collective action problems facing the relevant actors. I attempted to specify the transaction costs involved in each set of problems and assess the successes and failures at each level. What we found was a mixed record. For example, in many areas the tribes and the state have been quite successful at overcoming the substantial barriers to cooperation that were present when the regime was initially put into place. Those that remain are among the most difficult to solve for any cooperative endeavor. The remaining distrust *between* the state and the tribes has produced parallel systems for conducting research and carrying out some other management tasks. Yet an unintended consequence has been to *reduce* the costs associated with managing Indian fisheries by making scientific information and the regulations based on such information more credible.

Turning to intertribal relations, we find a number of institutions that allow the tribes to be quite successful in managing their relations with external actors. Tribes have created and maintain a supratribal organization that facilitates cooperation and allows them to present a united front on issues of shared concern. The organization also generates much of the systemwide data that the tribes use in negotiations with state, federal, and international management agencies as well as monitoring relevant political developments throughout the case area and handling many press contacts. All of these are functions more efficiently performed by a centralized agency, but which require a certain amount of mutual trust as well as the capacity to create structures that ensure accountability and evenhandedness. Tribes also cooperate in choosing representatives to sit on a variety of land and water-use advisory panels throughout the state. The overall result of tribal cooperation is that few major decisions regarding land use or water policy in the state are made without at least some consideration of tribal interests, which, in these areas, at least, are sufficiently homogeneous to be represented collectively.

With respect to solving collective action problems that arise in the context of interactions between tribes, there are both successes and failures. In addition to the supratribal organization discussed earlier, several smaller cooperatives perform some or all management functions for subsets of tribes that live in close proximity to one another. Among all tribes that share river systems there have evolved a variety of formal and informal agreements for handling joint management tasks and sharing allocation of some stocks. Even where the specific content of such agreements is regularly contested, the fact that there are forums for negotiating differences between tribes is significant and a necessary precondition for the resolution of differences. At the same time, there appear to be substantial unrealized gains from cooperation. For example, there were several allocational principles detailed in chapter 5 that would rank higher in terms of efficiency than those currently in use by the tribes, yet while the tribes are aware of them, they have not been adopted. Internal governance is a more complicated story, but here, too, there seem to be steps the tribes could take that would increase the aggregate wealth that their fishermen receive from fishing.

What stands in the way of the adoption of these more allocatively efficient institutions? It is quite clear that certain sorts of transaction costs, namely those associated with bargaining problems arising from distributive concerns, obstruct the adoption of more efficient institutions. As I argued in chapter 5, social actors are unwilling to agree to rules that would maximize aggregate wealth if they cannot be reached through Pareto superior moves. Unresolved distributional problems clearly block further steps in the direction of allocative efficiency.[4]

By comparison, consider again the circumstances at the time of Western contact with the aboriginal people of Puget Sound and the surrounding region. In chapter 2, I demonstrated that these institutions were highly efficient. How did this efficiency come about? Aboriginal institutions were allocatively efficient because social actors faced very low transaction costs due to a high degree of community among individuals and groups. Furthermore, participation in the practices that comprised these institutions helped sustain and strengthen these communities. Information about the preferences, reputations, and capabilities of various bargaining partners was relatively inexpensive to obtain, and people could expect that their interactions would go on into the indefinite future. Even more important was the fact that rules governing fishing and productive activities were

---

4. The fact that the distributional issues between tribes and the state have largely been resolved may explain why there is relatively more conflict (and less efficiency) in intertribal institutions than in state-tribal institutions. Although the tribes have greater regard for other tribes than for state managers, they also have a greater number of unsettled issues.

embedded in a complex of other institutions, many of which served to redistribute wealth. Parties could agree to wealth-maximizing rules because (1) there was a considerable chance that they themselves might now or in the future benefit from a given rule directly, and (2) a given share of the benefits of one individual's good fortune or hard work was redistributed to a network of relatives and fellow villagers. In this society, wealth really did trickle down. By solving the distribution problem, the Indians were able to solve the efficiency problem.

The fabric of redistributive institutions operating within and between tribes is much thinner today. Tribal members are less likely to intermarry, there is more economic inequality between them, and they are thus more likely to be affected unequally by a change in institutional arrangements. The barriers to allocatively efficient institutions are correspondingly larger.

But while distributional issues are paramount in the process by which individuals have created and reconfigured the institutions discussed in this study, these institutions are not merely the *by-products* of distributional conflicts. As is demonstrated at each of the levels discussed in chapters 4, 5, and 6, the actors are aware that they have a number of common as well as competing interests, and they actively consider how particular actions and the adoption of general principles will affect allocative efficiency and, indirectly, relations with each other.

Institutions reduce transaction costs, but they obviously do much more. In addition to helping social actors solve particular collective action problems or engage in exchange, the presence of and participation in institutions creates the preconditions for the formation of agreements and cooperative projects that otherwise would not even be contemplated. They are in this sense a resource that can be used in an incremental process by which groups "bootstrap" their way toward greater social cooperation. They expand the set of possibilities available to members of a group by providing them with opportunities to see how others may act or how particular rules may affect them. They also remind individuals that they are members of a particular group. It is in terms of these broader purposes that values such as equity or cultural identity animate the process of institutional design and change.

Tribal members and fisheries managers are clearly aware that fishing and the institutions that surround fisheries management are in some sense an affirmation of a shared identity and that they enhance the infrastructure of community. When the fishery manager for the Nisqually Tribe explains that it is the goal of the tribe to encourage tribal members to participate in fishing while discouraging fishermen from becoming economically dependent on the fishery, he is saying that at least in this tribe, the fisheries are valuable not only directly in economic terms but also for nurturing community. Similarly, the rule that all tribes have adopted that prioritizes ceremonial uses of salmon has the effect of continually reminding individuals that they are members of a larger community, thereby increasing the possibility that they will adopt cooperative strategies in other interactions. Intertribal ceremonies and festivals and the annual retreat for tribal and state managers perform much the same function at the level of intertribal and state-tribal relations, although obviously the connections here are somewhat weaker.

Finally, as this process of constructing and reconstructing the elaborate set of institutions that comprise this system of comanagement demonstrates, there was nothing inevitable about success in this case. Without the determination of tribal leaders to press for full exercise of their court-determined rights and the acumen of those who led the state Department of Fisheries in the mid-1980s and who were able to facilitate communication between the two sides and thus open the way to a more cooperative relationship, it is hard to believe that the system would have even survived, let alone become a model for other experiments with democratic governance and user-group management. Nor is success irreversible. Although the current system appears fairly robust, it is far from self-regulating. The system of management as well as the salmon themselves continue to demand careful stewardship.

References

A list of people interviewed for this study follows the references.

Acheson, James M. 1975. "The Lobster Fiefs: Economic and Ecological Effects of Territoriality in the Maine Lobster Industry." *Human Ecology* 3:183–207.
———. 1987. "The Lobster Fiefs, Revisited: Economic and Ecological Effects of Territoriality in the Maine Lobster Industry." In Bonnie J. McCay and James M. Acheson, eds., *The Question of the Commons,* 37–65. Tucson: University of Arizona Press.
Akerlof, George A. 1970. "The Market for 'Lemons': Quality, Uncertainty and the Market Mechanism." *Quarterly Journal of Economics* 84:488–500.
Alchian, Armen A., and Harold Demsetz. 1972. "Production, Information Costs and Economic Organization." *American Economic Review* 62:777–95.
Allen, Douglas W., and Dean Lueck. 1992. "The 'Back Forty' on a Handshake: Specific Assets, Reputation, and the Structure of Farmland Contracts." *Journal of Law, Economics and Organization* 8:366–76.
American Friends Service Committee. 1970. *Uncommon Controversy: Fishing Rights of the Muckleshoot, Puyallup and Nisqually Indians.* Seattle: University of Washington Press.
Andersen, Peder, and Jon G. Sutinen. 1985. "The Economics of Fisheries Law Enforcement." *Land Economics* 61:387–97.
Anderson, Terry L., and P. J. Hill. 1975. "The Evolution of Property Rights: A Study of the American West." *Journal of Law and Economics* 18:163–79.
Anderson, Terry L., and Donald R. Leal. *Free Market Environmentalism.* Boulder, CO: Westview Press.
Axelrod, Robert. 1981. "The Emergence of Cooperation among Egoists." *American Political Science Review* 75:305–18.
Baily, F. G. 1965. "Decision by Consensus in Councils and Committees: With Special Reference to Village and Local Government in India." In Michael Banton, ed., *Political Systems and the Distribution of Power.* London: Tavistock.
Baland, Jean-Marie, and Jean-Philippe Platteau. 1996. *Halting Degradation of Natural Resources: Is There a Role for Local Communities?* Oxford: Clarendon Press.
Barnett, Homer G. 1938. "The Coast Salish of Canada." *American Anthropologist* 40:118–41.
———. 1967. "The Nature of the Potlatch." In Tom McFeat, ed., *Indians of the North Pacific Coast.* Seattle: University of Washington Press.

Barsh, Russel L. 1977. *The Washington Fishing Rights Controversy: An Economic Critique.* Seattle: University of Washington, Graduate School of Business Administration.

———. 1982. "The Economics of a Traditional Coastal Indian Salmon Fishery." *Human Organization* 41:170–76.

———. 1991. "Backfire from Boldt: The Judicial Transformation of Coast Salish Proprietary Fisheries into a Commons." *Western Legal History* 4:85–102.

Barzel, Yoram. 1982. "Measurement Costs and the Organization of Markets." *Journal of Law and Economics* 25:27–48.

———. 1989. *Economic Analysis of Property Rights.* New York: Cambridge University Press.

Bates, Robert H. 1981. *Markets and States in Tropical Africa: The Political Basis of Agricultural Policies.* Berkeley: University of California Press.

Berkes, Fikret. 1986. "Marine Inshore Fishery Management in Turkey." In Proceedings of the Conference on Common Property Resource Management, National Research Council, 63–83. Washington DC: National Academy Press.

Boxberger, Daniel L. 1989. *To Fish in Common: The Ethnohistory of Lummi Indian Salmon Fishing.* Lincoln: University of Nebraska Press.

Brown, Bruce. 1982. *Mountain in the Clouds: A Search for the Wild Salmon.* New York: Simon and Schuster.

Brunn, Rita. 1982. "The Boldt Decision: Legal Victory, Political Defeat." *Law and Policy Quarterly* 4:271–86.

Cheung, Steven N. S. 1970. "The Structure of a Contract and the Theory of a Non-Exclusive Resource." *Natural Resources Journal* 15:713–27.

Ciriacy-Wantrup, S. V., and Bishop, R. C. 1975. "'Common Property' as a Concept in Natural Resource Policy." *Natural Resources Journal* 15:713–27.

Clark, C. W. 1977. "The Economics of Over-Exploitation." In Garrett Hardin and John Baden, eds., *Managing the Commons,* 82–95. San Francisco: Freeman.

Clark, William G. 1985. "Fishing in a Sea of Court Orders: Puget Sound Salmon Management Ten Years after the Boldt Decision." *North American Journal of Fisheries Management* 5:417–34.

Coase, Ronald H. 1937. "The Nature of the Firm." *Economica* 4:386–405.

———. 1960. "The Problem of Social Cost." *Journal of Law and Economics* 3:1–44.

Codere, Helen. 1967. "Fighting with Property: A Study of Kwakiutl Potlatching and Warfare 1792–1930." In Tom McFeat, ed., *Indians of the North Pacific Coast,* 92–111. Seattle: University of Washington Press.

Cohen, Fay G. 1986. *Treaties on Trial: The Continuing Controversy over Northwest Indian Fishing Rights.* Seattle: University of Washington Press.

Colemen, Jules L. 1988. *Markets, Morals and the Law.* New York: Cambridge University Press.

———. 1992. *Risks and Wrongs.* New York: Cambridge University Press.

Coleman, Jules L., Douglas D. Heckathorn, and Steven M. Maser. 1989. "A Bargaining Theory Approach to Default Provisions and Disclosure Rules in Contract Law." *Harvard Journal of Law and Public Policy* 12:639–709.

Collins, June M. 1950. "Growth of Class Distinctions and Political Authority among the Skagit Indians during the Contact Period." *American Anthropologist* 52:331–42.

Cordell, John, ed. 1989. *A Sea of Small Boats.* Cambridge, MA: Cultural Survival, Inc.

Crutchfield, James A., and Giulio Pontecorvo. 1969. "The Pacific Salmon Fisheries: A Study of Irrational Conservation." Baltimore: John Hopkins University Press.

Dahlman, Carl J. 1979. "The Problem of Externality." *Journal of Law and Economics* 22:141–62.

———. 1980. *The Open Field System and Beyond: A Property Rights Analysis of an Economic Institution.* Cambridge: Cambridge University Press.

Dasgupta, Partha S. 1982. *The Control of Resources.* Cambridge: Harvard University Press.

Demsetz, Harold. 1967. "Toward a Theory of Property Rights." *American Economic Review* 57:347–59.

Drucker, Philip. 1951. "The Northern and Central Nootkan Tribes." *Bureau of American Ethnology Bulletin* 144. U.S. Government Printing Office.

———. 1967. "Some Variations on the Potlatch." In Tom McFeat, ed. *Indians of the North Pacific Coast.* Seattle: University of Washington Press.

Dyson-Hudson, Rada, and Eric Alden Smith. 1978. "Human Territoriality: An Ecological Reassessment." *American Anthropologist* 80:21–41.

Eggertsson, Thrainn. 1990. *Economic Behavior and Institutions.* New York: Cambridge University Press.

Ellickson, Robert C. 1989. "A Hypothesis of Wealth-Maximizing Norms: Evidence from the Whaling Industry." *Journal of Law, Economics and Organization* 5:83–97.

———. 1991. *Order without Law: How Neighbors Settle Disputes.* Cambridge: Harvard University Press.

Feeny, David, Fikret Berkes, Bonnie J. McCay, and James M. Acheson. 1990. "The Tragedy of the Commons: Twenty-Two Years Later." *Human Ecology* 18:1–19.

Ferguson, R. Brian. 1983. "Warfare and Redistributive Exchange on the Northwest Coast." In Elizabeth Tooker, ed., *The Development of Political Organization in Native North America,* 133–47. Philadelphia: American Ethnological Society.

———. 1984. *Warfare, Culture and Environment.* Orlando, FL: Academic Press.

Fraidenburg, Michael E. 1989. "The New Politics of Natural Resources: Negotiating a Shift Toward Privatization of Natural Resource Policymaking in Washington State." *Northwest Environmental Journal* 5:211–40.

Frolich, Norman, and Joel A. Oppenheimer. 1978. *Modern Political Economy.* Englewood Cliffs, NJ: Prentice-Hall.

Gordon, H. Scott. 1954. "The Economic Theory of a Common Property Resource: The Fishery." *Journal of Political Economy* 62 (2): 124–42.

Halpert, Cynthia, and Kai Lee. 1990. "The Timber, Fish and Wildlife Agreement:

154   References

Implementing Alternative Dispute Resolution in Washington State." *Northwest Environmental Journal* 6 (2): 139–75.

Hanna, Susan S., Carl Folke, and Karl-Goran Maler. 1996. *Rights to Nature: Ecological, Economic, Cultural, and Political Principles of Institutions for the Environment.* Washington, DC: Island Press.

Hardin, Garrett. 1968. "The Tragedy of the Commons." *Science* 162:1243–48.

Hardin, Russell. 1982. *Collective Action.* Baltimore: John Hopkins University Press.

Heckathorn, Douglas D., and Steven M. Maser. 1987. "Bargaining and the Sources of Transaction Costs: The Case of Government Regulation." *Journal of Law, Economics and Organization* 3:69–98.

Hewes, Gordon W. 1973. *Indian Fisheries Productivity in Pre-Contact Times in the Pacific Salmon Area.* Northwest Anthropological Research Notes 7:133–55.

Higgs, Robert. 1982. "Legally Induced Technical Regress in the Washington Salmon Fishery." *Research in Economic History* 7:55–86.

Huntington, Charles, Willa Nehlson, and Jon Bowers. 1996. "A Survey of Healthy Native Stocks of Anadromous Salmonids in the Pacific Northwest and California." *Fisheries* 21 (3): 6–14.

Huppert, D. D., and M. W. Odemar. 1986. "A Review of California's Limited Entry Program." In Nina Mollett, ed., *Fishery Access Control Programs Worldwide: Proceedings of the Workshop on Management Options for the North Pacific Longline Fisheries,* Alaska Sea Grant Report 86, no. 4, 301–12.

Johnsen, D. Bruce. 1986. "The Formation and Protection of Property Rights among the Southern Kwakiutl Indians." *Journal of Legal Studies* 15:41–67.

Johnson, Ronald N., and Gary D. Libecap. 1982. "Contracting Problems and Regulation: The Case of the Fishery." *American Economic Review* 72: 1005–22.

Knight, Jack. 1992. *Institutions and Social Conflict.* New York: Cambridge University Press.

———. 1995. "Models, Interpretations, and Theories: Constructing Explanations of Institutional Emergence and Change." In Jack Knight and Itai Sened, eds., *Explaining Social Institutions.* Ann Arbor: University of Michigan Press.

Knight, Jack, and Itai Sened, eds. 1995. *Explaining Social Institutions.* Ann Arbor: University of Michigan Press.

Lane, Barbara. 1973. "Political and Economic Aspects of Indian-White Culture Contact in Western Washington in Mid-19th Century." *United States Exhibits 20–30, U.S. v. Washington.* 384 F. Supp. 312.

Levi, Margaret. 1988. *Of Rule and Revenue.* Berkeley: University of California Press.

Libecap, Gary D. 1989. *Contracting for Property Rights.* New York: Cambridge University Press.

Ludwig, Donald, Ray Hilborn, and Carl Wallace. 1993. "Uncertainty, Resource Exploitation, and Conservation: Lessons from History." *Science* 260:17, 36.

Madson, Pamela K., and William Koss. 1988. *Washington Salmon: Understanding Salmon Allocation.* Olympia: Office of Program Research, House of Representatives, State of Washington.

Mayhew, David R. 1974. *Congress: The Electoral Connection.* New Haven, CT: Yale University Press.

McCay, Bonnie J., and James M. Acheson, eds. 1987. *The Question of the Commons: The Culture and Ecology of Communal Resources.* Tucson: University of Arizona Press.

McCubbins, Mathew D., and T. Schwartz. 1984. "Congressional Oversight Overlooked: Police Patrols versus Fire Alarms." *American Journal of Political Science* 28:165–79.

McKean, Margaret A. 1982. "The Japanese Experience with Scarcity: Management of Traditional Common Lands." *Environmental Review* 6 (2): 63–88.

———. 1986. "Management of Traditional Common Lands (Iriaichi) in Japan." In National Research Council, *Proceedings of the Conference on Common-Property Resource Management,* 533–89. Washington, DC: National Academy Press.

Miller, Gary J. 1992. *Managerial Dilemmas: The Political Economy of Hierarchy.* New York: Cambridge University Press.

Moe, Terry M. 1984. "The New Economics of Organization." *American Journal of Political Science* 28:165–79.

Morishima, Gary. 1987. "Native American Artisanal Fisheries Management in the Pacific Northwest: A Piece of the Pie." Unpublished paper.

Natural Resources Law Institute, Lewis and Clark Law School. 1990. *Anadromous Fish Law Memo* 50.

Netboy, Anthony. 1974. *The Salmon: Their Fight for Survival.* Boston: Houghton Mifflin.

Netting, Robert McC. 1981. *Balancing on an Alp.* New York: Cambridge University Press.

———. 1982. "Territory, Property, and Tenure." In Robert McAdams, Neil J. Smelser, and Donald J. Treiman, eds. *Behavioral and Social Science Research: A National Resource,* 446–501. Washington, DC: National Academy Press.

Northwest Indian Fisheries Commission (NWIFC). 1990. "Comprehensive Tribal Fisheries Management: A Holistic Approach."

North, Douglass C. 1981. *Structure and Change in Economic History.* New York: Norton.

Nozick, Robert. 1974. *Anarchy, State and Utopia.* New York: Basic Books.

Okun, Arthur M. 1975. *Equality and Efficiency: The Big Tradeoff.* Washington, DC: Brookings Institution.

Olson, Mancur. 1965. *The Logic of Collective Action.* Cambridge: Harvard University Press.

Onats, Astrida R. Blukis. 1984. "The Interaction of Kin, Marriage, Property Ownership, and Residence with Respect to Resource Locations among the Coast Salish of the Puget Lowland." *Northwest Anthropological Research Notes,* vol. 18, no. 1: 86–96. Moscow, ID: Department of Sociology/Anthropology, University of Idaho.

Ostrom, Elinor. 1990. *Governing the Commons: The Evolution of Institutions for Collective Action.* New York: Cambridge University Press.

Ostrom, Elinor, Roy Gardner, and James Walker. 1994. *Rules, Games and Common-Pool Resources.* Ann Arbor: University of Michigan Press.

Piddocke, Stuart. 1965. "The Potlatch System of the Southern Kwakiutl: A New Perspective." *Southwestern Journal of Anthropology* 21:244–64.

Pinkerton, Evelyn, ed. 1989. *Cooperative Management of Local Fisheries: New Directions for Improved Management and Community Development.* Vancouver: University of British Columbia Press.

Pinkerton, Evelyn, and Nelson Keitlah. 1990. "The Point No Point Treaty Council: Innovation by an Inter-Tribal Fisheries Management Cooperative." University of British Columbia Planning Papers Series no. 26, School of Community and Regional Planning, University of British Columbia, Vancouver.

Popkin, Samuel L. 1979. *The Rational Peasant: The Political Economy of Rural Society in Vietnam.* Berkeley: University of California Press.

Posner, Richard A. 1977. *Economic Analysis of Law.* Boston: Little, Brown.

———. 1980. "A Theory of Primitive Society, with Special Reference to Law." *Journal of Law and Economics* 23:1–53.

Rae, Douglas. 1979. "The Egalitarian State: Notes on a Contradictory System of Ideals." *Daedalus* 108, no. 4 (fall 1979): 37–54.

Rae, Douglas, and Douglas Yates et al. 1981. *Equalities.* Cambridge: Harvard University Press.

Rawls, John. 1971. *A Theory of Justice.* Cambridge: Harvard University Press.

Richardson, Allan. 1981. "The Control of Productive Resources on the Northwest Coast of North America." In Nancy M. Williams and Eugene S. Hunn, eds., *Resource Managers: North American and Australian Hunter-Gatherers,* 93–112. Boulder, CO: Westview Press.

Romanoff, Steven. 1985. *Fraser Lillooet Indian Fishing.* Northwest Anthropological Research Notes, vol. 19.

Roos, John F. 1991. *Restoring Fraser River Salmon: A History of the International Pacific Salmon Fisheries Commission, 1937–1985.* Vancouver, BC: Pacific Salmon Commission.

Royce, William F., Donald E. Bevan, James A. Crutchfield, Gerald J. Paulik, and Robert L. Fletcher. 1963. "Salmon Gear Limitation in Northern Washington Waters: An Economic, Biological, and Legal Survey of the Salmon Resource of Northern Puget Sound and Strait of Juan de Fuca." *Contribution No. 145.* College of Fisheries, University of Washington, Seattle, Washington.

Seiter, Ann E. 1993. "Putting Process into Practice: Tribal Leadership in Regional Water Planning." Paper presented at the American Water Resource Association Summer Symposium on Changing Roles in Water Resources Management and Policy, 27–30 June, Seattle.

Shelley, Peter, Jennifer Atkinson, Eleanor Dorsey, and Priscilla Brooks. 1996. "The New England Fisheries Crisis: What Have We Learned?" *Tulane Environmental Law Journal* 9:221–44.

Shepsle, Kenneth A., and Barry R. Weingast. 1981. "Structure-Induced Equilibrium and Legislative Choice." *Public Choice* 37:503–19.

Singh, Ram Raj Prasad. 1966. *Aboriginal Economic Systems of the Olympic Penin-*

sula Indians, Western Washington. Sacramento, CA: Sacramento Anthropological Society.

Singleton, Sara, and Michael Taylor. 1992. "Common Property, Collective Action and Community." *Journal of Theoretical Politics* 4:309–24.

Skocpol, Theda. 1979. *States and Social Revolutions: A Comparative Analysis of France, Russia and China.* New York: Cambridge University Press.

Stern, Bernhard J. 1934. *The Lummi Indians of Northwest Washington.* New York: Columbia University Press.

Stevenson, Glenn. 1991. *Common Property Economics: A General Theory and Land Use Application.* Cambridge: Cambridge University Press.

Stone, Deborah A. 1988. *Policy Paradox and Political Reason.* New York: Harper-Collins.

Suttles, Wayne. 1987. *Coast Salish Essays.* Seattle: University of Washington Press.

Swan, James G. 1870. *The Indians of Cape Flattery, at the Entrance to the Strait of Fuca, Washington Territory.* Smithsonian Contributions to Knowledge vol.6, article 8, no. 220.

Taylor, Michael. 1976. *Anarchy and Cooperation.* London: John Wiley.

———. 1982. *Community, Anarchy and Liberty.* New York: Cambridge University Press.

———. 1987. *The Possibility of Cooperation.* New York: Cambridge University Press.

Taylor, Michael, and Sara Singleton. 1993. "The Communal Resource: Transaction Costs and the Solution of Collective Action Problems." *Politics and Society* 21:195–214.

Townsend, Ralph. 1990. "Entry Restrictions in the Fishery: A Survey of the Evidence." *Land Economics* 66:359–78.

Tsebelis, George. 1990. *Nested Games.* Berkeley: University of California Press.

Umbeck, John R. 1981. "Might Makes Rights: A Theory of the Formation and Initial Distribution of Property Rights." *Economic Inquiry* 20:38–59.

Waldo, James. 1981. *U.S. v. Washington, Phase II: Analysis and Recommendations.* Prepared for the Northwest Water Resources Committee, Seattle.

Washington State Department of Fisheries. 1924–27, 1956–72, 1990a. *Annual Reports.* Olympia: State Government Printing Office.

———. 1956–62, 1989, 1990b. *Fisheries Statistical Report.* Olympia: State Government Printing Office.

———. 1977–79. *Technical Reports,* nos. 25, 26, 27, 40, 44, 47. Olympia: State Government Printing Office.

———. 1991. "A Study of Washington's Commercial Fisheries." Prepared in Compliance with Substitute Senate Bill 5501.

———. 1993. *Washington State Sport Catch Report 1991.* Olympia: State Government Printing Office.

Washington State Department of Fish and Wildlife. 1995. *Washington State Sport Catch Report for Foodfish.* Olympia: State Government Printing Office.

————. 1996. *Fisheries Statistical Report.* Olympia: State Government Printing Office.

Waterman, Thomas T. 1920. *The Whaling Equipment of the Makah Indians.* Seattle: University of Washington Publications in Political and Social Science, vol. 1, no. 1.

Weber, Max. 1930. *The Protestant Ethic and the Spirit of Capitalism.* London: Allen and Unwin.

Weingast, Barry R., and William J. Marshall. 1988. "The Industrial Organization of Congress; or, Why Legislatures, Unlike Firms, Are Not Organized as Markets." *Journal of Political Economy* 96:132–63.

Weingast, Barry R., and Mark J. Moran. 1983. "Bureaucratic Discretion or Legislative Control? Regulatory Policymaking by the Federal Trade Commission." *Journal of Political Economy* 91:765–800.

Wilkinson, Charles. 1987. *Crossing the Next Meridian.* Washington, DC: Island Press.

Williamson, Oliver F. 1975. *Markets and Hierarchies: Analysis and Antitrust Implications.* New York: Free Press.

————. 1983. "Credible Commitment: Using Hostages to Support Exchange." *American Economic Review* 74: 519–40.

————. 1985. *The Economic Implications of Capitalism: Firms, Markets and Relational Contracting.* New York: Free Press.

Wilson, James A., James M. Acheson, Mark Metcalfe, and Peter Kleban. 1994. "Chaos, Complexity and Community Management of Fisheries." *Marine Policy* 18:291–305.

Wold, Timothy Michael. 1989. "After the Boldt Decision: The Question of Inter-Tribal Allocation." Master's thesis, University of Washington.

Yanagida, Joy A. 1987. "The Pacific Salmon Treaty." *American Journal of International Law* 81:577–92.

Interviews

Anonymous Washington State Department of Fisheries biologist, identified as Interview A. Olympia.

Anonymous Squaxin Island fishermen. Shelton, WA. March 2, 1993.

Bohl, Martin. Head of Code Writing Department, Northwest Intertribal Court System, Edmonds, WA. March 16, 1994.

Coons, Jim. Pacific Fisheries Management Council, Portland, OR. August 28, 1992.

Cooper, Harry Jr. Fisherman and former fisheries manager, Nooksack Tribe, Deming, WA. August 15, 1993.

Davis, Bob. Department of Fisheries, Lummi Indian Nation, Bellingham, WA. September 21, 1993.

DiDonato, Gene. Harvest Management Division, Washington State Department of Fisheries, Olympia. January 6, 1993.

Evenhuis, Lee. Natural resources director, Squaxin Island Tribe, Shelton, WA. March 2, 1993.

Fraidenburg, Michael. Washington State Department of Fisheries, Olympia. December 16, 1992.

Freeman, Judith. Deputy director for resource management, Washington Department of Fisheries, Olympia. December 21, 1992.

Gilbert, Pauley. Chairman, Fisheries Advisory Board, Department of Fisheries, University of Washington, Seattle. April 16, 1992.

Graves, Gary. Northwest Indian Fisheries Commission, Olympia, WA. July 29, 1992.

Griggs, Dale. Fisheries manager, Nooksack Tribe, Deming, WA. August 10, 1993.

Hage, Paul. Fisheries manager, Muckleshoot Tribe, Auburn, WA. February 9, 1993.

Harp, James. Natural resources director, Quinault Indian Nation; tribal representative on Pacific Fishery Management Council and commissioner on Northwest Indian Fisheries Commission. April 1, 1994.

Harris, Harold. Chairman of Puyallup Tribal Fish Commission, Puyallup, WA. February 5, 1993.

Huppert, Daniel. Professor, Department of Marine Affairs, University of Washington, Seattle. February 18, 1992.

James, Gerald I. General manager, Lummi Nation, Bellingham, WA. March 23, 1994.

Jorgenson, James. Fisheries manager, Hoh Tribe, Forks, WA. April 1, 1994.

Joseph, Lawrence. Fisheries manager, Sauk-Suiattle Tribe, Darrington, WA. July 11, 1992.

Lampsakis, Nicholas. Point No Point Treaty Council, Port Gamble, WA. August 21, 1993.

Loomis, Lorraine. Pacific Salmon Treaty commissioner and fisheries manager, Swinomish Tribe, La Conner, WA. October 4, 1993.

Lutz, Keith. Northwest Indian Fisheries Commission, Olympia, WA. July 15, 1992.

Manary, Edward. Legislative liaison, Washington State Department of Fisheries, Olympia. January 6, 1993.

Mathews, Dana. Enforcement Division, Washington State Department of Fisheries, Olympia. January 6, 1993.

Pattillo, Pat. Washington State Department of Fisheries, Olympia. December 16, 1992.

Peck, Larry. Enhancement Division, Washington State Department of Fisheries, Olympia. December 21, 1992.

Rutter, Larry. Northwest Indian Fisheries Commission, Olympia, WA. September 15, 1993.

Scott, Teresa. Washington State Department of Fisheries, Olympia. January 11, 1993.

Seiter, Ann E. Natural resources director, Jamestown S'Kallam Tribe, Sequim, WA. September 20, 1993.

Sekulich, Paul. Habitat and Enhancement Division, Washington State Department of Fisheries, Olympia. January 6, 1993.

Sele, Brad. Fisheries manager, Jamestown S'Klallam Tribe, Sequim, WA. September 20, 1993.

Troutt, David. Fisheries manager, Nisqually Tribe, Olympia, WA. February 9, 1993.

Turner, Robert. 1993. Washington State Department of Fisheries, Olympia. January 11, 1993.

Warren, William. Fisheries manager, Puyallup Tribe, Tacoma, WA. February 5, 1993.

Williams, Bruce. Fisheries manager, Port Gamble S'Klallam Tribe, Kingston, WA. August 21, 1992.

Wright, Frank Jr. Fisherman and fish commissioner, Puyallup Tribe, Tacoma, WA. February 5, 1993.

Index